böhlau

QUELLEN UND DARSTELLUNGEN
ZUR HANSISCHEN GESCHICHTE

HERAUSGEGEBEN
VOM
HANSISCHEN GESCHICHTSVEREIN

NEUE FOLGE / BAND LXXIX

Stephen H. Rigby / Robert C. Nash

The Overseas Trade of Boston, 1279–1548

BÖHLAU VERLAG WIEN KÖLN

Published with financial support from the Marc Fitch Fund.

MARC FITCH FUND

Bibliographic information published by the Deutsche Nationalbibliothek:
The Deutsche Nationalbibliothek lists this publication in the Deutsche Nationalbibliografie;
detailed bibliographic data available online: https://dnb.de

Koninklijke Brill NV incorporates the imprints Brill, Brill Nijhoff, Brill Hotei,
Brill Schöningh, Brill Fink, Brill mentis, Vandenhoeck & Ruprecht,
Böhlau, Verlag Antike, V&R unipress and Wageningen Academic.

Cover image: St Botolph's parish church, Boston, with the Stump
(14th to early 16th centuries) © Stephen H. Rigby

Cover design: Michael Haderer, Vienna
Proofreading: Cynthia Peck-Kubaczek, Vienna
Typesetting: buero mn, Bielefeld
Druck und Bindung: ⊕ Hubert & Co. BuchPartner, Göttingen
Printed in the EU

Vandenhoeck & Ruprecht Verlage | www.vandenhoeck-ruprecht-verlage.com

ISBN 978-3-412-52658-0

Contents

Preface

The particular and enrolled accounts of the customs and subsidies levied on England's medieval trade which are preserved amongst the records of the royal Exchequer provide us with a picture of English commerce in the later Middle Ages that is unparalleled in its detail and richness. These sources are particularly important for the study of the history of the Lincolnshire town of Boston, which, despite being one of England's largest towns and major ports in the thirteenth and fourteenth centuries, lacks a borough archive of the kind that allows us to trace the history of many of England's other medieval towns. Nevertheless, although the present study outlines some of the major changes in the composition of Boston's overseas trade as revealed by the customs accounts, its purpose is not to offer a detailed description or explanation of the development of the port's commerce in this period: I hope to provide a more in-depth analysis of Boston's trade in a future account of the town's history in the later Middle Ages. Rather, the aim of this study is to bring together all of the statistical data from Boston's enrolled customs accounts for the period from 1279 to 1548 so as to trace the fluctuations in the volume of the port's commerce, the changes in the nature of the commodities which were imported and exported, and the shifts in the origin of the merchants who shipped them (whether denizen or alien, Hansard or non-Hanseatic alien), and to explain the evolution of the customs system which produced this information. I hope that this book might inspire specialists in the history of other ports to publish similar studies so that we will eventually have detailed and comprehensive statistical information available for the medieval trade of each of England's customs' head ports during this period.

All historical research is necessarily a collaborative exercise. In writing this book, I have benefitted from assistance generously provided by Jim Bolton, Bruce Campbell, John Oldland and Alex Sapoznik. I am also very grateful to Mark Bailey, Rosalind Brown-Grant, Pamela Cawthorne and Wendy Childs for their extremely useful feedback on earlier drafts, and to Cath D'Alton who prepared Map 1. I am especially indebted to Stuart Jenks and Maryanne Kowaleski for their expert advice and detailed guidance on England's trade and customs system, and to Robert Nash who not only suggested many improvements to my text but also prepared the graphs of Boston's imports and exports given below. Naturally, none of these scholars can be held responsible for the errors which inevitably remain in the text. Finally, particular thanks are owed to the trustees of the Marc Fitch Fund for providing the financial support which enabled the publication of this book.

Stephen H. Rigby

List of figures (tables and graphs)

1.

The Exchequer enrolled customs accounts as a source for English overseas trade in the later Middle Ages

Modern visitors to the Lincolnshire town of Boston are likely to be struck by the surviving architectural evidence of the town's wealth and importance in the Middle Ages. Its existing medieval buildings include the Guildhall, which dates from the 1390s, the refectory of the Dominican friary (the only one of Boston's four mendicant houses with standing remains), a number of brick and timber-framed domestic buildings and, most famously of all, St Botolph's, which is one of the largest medieval parish churches in England and whose famous tower, the Stump, is the highest in England (excluding spires).[1] Around the time that the Guildhall was being built for the Guild of the Blessed Virgin Mary, Boston was amongst the leading urban communities in the country, with its 1377 poll tax return suggesting a population of perhaps 5,500, the tenth largest of any town in England.[2] Yet, disappointingly, the surviving written sources for medieval Boston are scattered and fragmentary. Despite its size and importance, medieval Boston did not achieve the formal self-government enjoyed by many other English towns, especially royal towns such as Lincoln or Grimsby, which were administered by their own elected officials and which have their own borough archives. Instead, Boston was subject to

1 For these buildings, see G. Harden, *Medieval Boston and its Archaeological Implications* (Sleaford, 1978); J. Minnis and K. Carmichael, *Boston, Lincolnshire: Historic North Sea Port and Market Town* (Swindon, 2015); K. Giles, 'St Mary's Guildhall, Boston, Lincolnshire: the archaeology of a medieval "public" building', *Medieval Archaeology*, 55 (2011), pp. 226–56; S. Moorhouse, 'Finds in the refectory at the Dominican friary, Boston', *Lincolnshire History and Archaeology*, 7 (1972), pp. 21–53; L. Monckton, '"The beste and fayrest of al Lincolnshire": the parish church of St Botolph, Boston', in S. Badham and P. Cockerham, eds, *'The beste and fayrest of al Lincolnshire': The Church of St Botolph's, Boston, Lincolnshire, and its Medieval Monuments* (British Archaeological Reports, British Series, 554 (2012)), pp. 29–48. For further reading on medieval Boston, see the notes and bibliography in S. H. Rigby, *Boston, 1086–1225: A Medieval Boom Town* (Lincoln, 2017).

2 The National Archives, London (T.N.A.), Exchequer LT.R., Enrolled Lay Subsidy Returns, E359/8B, m. 18; E359/8C; *The Poll Taxes of 1377, 1379 and 1381, Part 2: Lincolnshire-Westmoreland*, ed. C. Fenwick (Oxford, 2001), p. 3. For the problems involved in calculating total populations from numbers of taxpayers in 1377, see S. H. Rigby, 'Urban population in late medieval England: the evidence of the lay subsidies', *Economic History Review*, 63 (2010), pp. 393–417, at 398–9. For urban populations in 1377, see A. Dyer, 'Ranking lists of English medieval towns', in D. M. Palliser, ed., *The Cambridge Urban History of Britain*, Volume I (Cambridge, 2000), pp. 747–70, at 758.

the overlordship of a number of different manorial administrations; consequently a dedicated borough archive has not survived for the period before the town's incorporation in 1545.[3]

As a result, perhaps the most important surviving sources for Boston's history in the later Middle Ages—and certainly the most significant quantitative sources—are not borough records, but rather the accounts of the royal customs and subsidies levied on the port's overseas trade as part of the national customs system which was developed by the Crown from 1275 onwards. At first, only exports of wool, woolfells and hides were customed but, over the course of the fourteenth century, more and more commodities were brought into the system until, by the end of the century, virtually every import or export was subject to one or more duties.[4] The officials who collected these customs were responsible for accounting at the royal Exchequer for the revenues from the overseas trade which was carried out within their jurisdiction.[5] Two main forms of accounts survive as the products of this system and together they provide us with evidence for England's overseas trade whose detail is unparalleled in the rest of medieval Europe. First are the detailed 'particular' customs accounts produced by the local customs officials themselves which were sent to the royal Exchequer to be audited. These accounts list the individual ships which arrived at or left a port within a specific period, often that of the Exchequer year which ran from Michaelmas (29 September) to Michaelmas, along with the names of the merchants with goods on board and details of the commodities they imported and exported.[6] The particular accounts, whether compiled by the customs collectors themselves (in which case they also give details of the customs and

3 S. H. Rigby, 'Boston and Grimsby in the Middle Ages: an administrative contrast', *Journal of Medieval History*, 10 (1984), pp. 51–66; S. H. Rigby, *Medieval Grimsby: Growth and Decline* (Hull, 1993), chapters 2, 4. For the text of Boston's 1545 charter of incorporation, see T. H. Allen, *The History of the County of Lincoln from the Earliest Period to the Present Time* (two volumes; London, 1834), I: 233–8. Allen ascribed the charter to 1546 (*Ibid.*, pp. 226, 238), as did Thompson (P. Thompson, *The History and Antiquities of Boston* (Boston, 1856), p. 64) and, following him, some recent popular histories of the town, but the charter was actually dated 14 May, 37 Henry VIII, i.e. 1545 (*Letters and Papers, Foreign and Domestic, of the Reign of Henry VIII*, volume 20, part 1, no. 846/38; *British Borough Charters, 1307–1660*, ed. M. Weinbaum (Cambridge, 1943), pp. 69–70).

4 For the evolution of the customs administration, see N. S. B. Gras, *The Early English Customs System* (Cambridge, Mass., 1918).

5 For the accounting procedure, see *The Overseas Trade of London: Exchequer Customs Accounts, 1480–1*, ed. H. S. Cobb (London Record Society, 27 (1990)), pp. xxiv–xxviii; *The London Customs Accounts: 24 Henry VI (1445/46)*, ed. S. Jenks (Cologne, 2018), pp. xxiv–lx.

6 T.N.A., Exchequer K. R. Customs Accounts, E122. For the text of particular accounts for Boston, see *The Overseas Trade of Boston in the Reign of Richard II*, ed. S. H. Rigby (Lincoln Record Society, 93, (2005)); Gras, *The Early English Customs System*, pp. 273–302, 516–20; and the Appendix below.

subsidies due from each merchant and of the total amount owed to the Exchequer) or by the controller, who was appointed in each port as a check on the collectors' honesty and efficiency, are unrivalled in their detail. Unfortunately, however, once the Exchequer accounting procedure was completed, there was little need to preserve these accounts and so their survival in all ports is rather random and very patchy. For instance, for Boston, we have particular accounts for only eight of the twenty-two years of Richard II's reign (1377–99).[7]

By contrast, the second form of the customs accounts, the 'enrolled' accounts compiled at the Exchequer itself, do survive for most years from 1279 to 1548. These accounts summarise the volume or value of trade liable to each particular duty in each port within a specific accounting period and record the total amounts of custom and subsidy due from each of them for which the collectors were liable at the Exchequer. As a result, the enrolled accounts allow us to follow the annual fluctuations in the trade of individual ports—and of England as a whole—in the later Middle Ages. Since merchants of different origins paid customs and subsidies at variable rates, it is often possible to distinguish the trade of denizen (mainly English-born) merchants from those of alien merchants, or to separate the trade of merchants of the Hanseatic League from that of other aliens.[8] Before 1303, these enrolled accounts were included alongside other forms of royal income in the Exchequer pipe rolls, but after this date the enrolled accounts of revenues from customs and subsidies on overseas trade were gathered together in separate rolls.[9]

Within the customs system, Boston was one of the 'head ports' (of which there were thirteen in the fourteenth century, and fifteen or sixteen in the following century) whose officials were responsible for collecting customs along particular stretches of the English coastline.[10] The Boston collectors' authority stretched northwards along the Lincolnshire coast to Grimsby, which sometimes lay within the jurisdiction of the Hull collectors and sometimes in that of Boston, and to the south extended either to Maidenhouse (a deserted port now in Clenchwarton parish, Norfolk) or to Wisbech (Cambridgeshire), where the Lynn customs jurisdiction began (see Map 1).[11] The enrolled customs accounts rarely distinguish

7 Rigby, *The Overseas Trade of Boston in the Reign of Richard II*, pp. xvii–xviii.

8 Although most denizens were native-born Englishmen, this category also included foreign merchants who had received letters patent granting them denizen status. For instance, Henry Kerle, a German merchant, was awarded this status in 1385 (*Calendar of Patent Rolls, 1381–85*, p. 581), as was Herman Standforth in 1390 (*Calendar of Patent Rolls, 1388–92*, p. 367).

9 T.N.A. Pipe Rolls, E372/124–5; E372/133–4; E372/146; E372/149; T.N.A., Exchequer L.T.R. Enrolled Customs Accounts, E356/1–27; *The Enrolled Customs Accounts, Parts 1–12*, ed. S. Jenks (List and Index Society, volumes 303, 306–7, 313–14, 319, 324, 334, 341, 344–5, 348 (2004–13)).

10 M. Kowaleski, 'Port towns: England and Wales, 1300–1540', in Palliser, *Cambridge Urban History of Britain*, I, pp. 467–94, at 472; Jenks, *London Customs Accounts*, p. xviii.

11 E. M. Carus-Wilson and O. Coleman, *England's Export Trade, 1275–1547* (Oxford, 1963), pp. 178, 187–8.

Boston's member-ports from that of Boston itself, but when they do so they show that their trade was extremely minor compared with that of the head port itself. For instance, for the period from March 1347 to April 1348, the collectors of a subsidy on overseas trade levied in Grimsby and its nearby villages of Clee and Itterby (see Map 1) reported that no wool exports had been made there and that the value of other goods imported and exported there amounted to only £ 108 10s. whereas the Boston collectors accounted for the subsidy on over 3,837 sacks of wool exports and on £ 3,608 of other goods in the same period.[12] Similarly, from 16 November 1378 to 27 May 1379, the Grimsby collectors of a subsidy of poundage levied at 6d. in the pound of the value of imports and exports, excluding wool, woolfells, hides and wine, accounted for the revenue collected from only £ 82 13s. 4d. of imports and exports made in the port, less than 1% of the £ 10,172 6s. 11d. of goods liable to the subsidy which passed through Boston during the same period.[13]

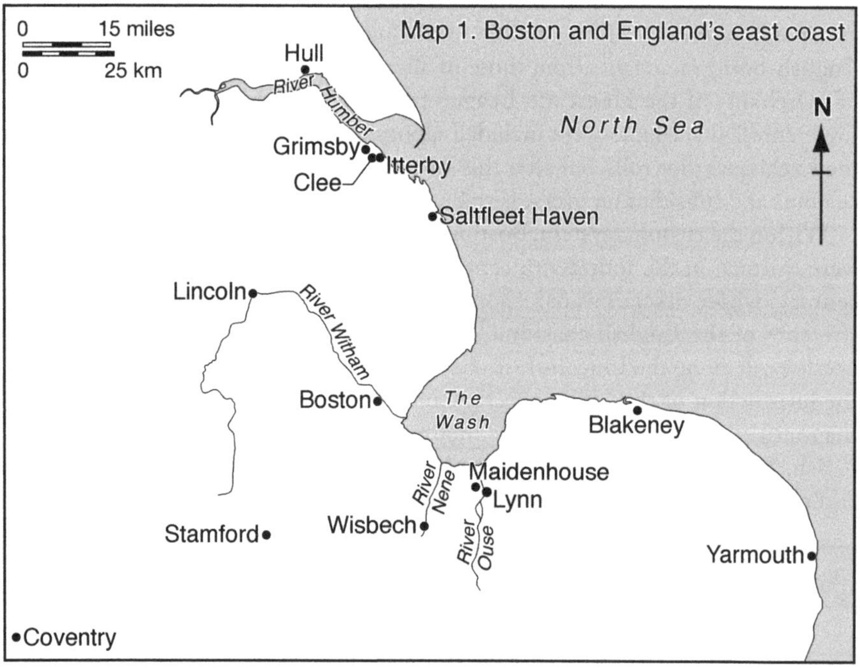

Map of Boston and England's east coast

12 T.N.A., E356/5, mm. 10, 12, 12d. See also E356/5, mm. 23, 23d.

13 T.N.A., E356/5, m. 23d; E356/13, m. 1d; *Calendar of Fine Rolls, 1377–81*, p. 121. See also Rigby, *Overseas Trade of Boston*, p. xvi; T.N.A., E356/9, mm. 24, 24d. For the scale of Grimsby's overseas trade, see Rigby, *Medieval Grimsby*, pp. 56–7.

Unfortunately, with only a few exceptions, the particular customs accounts also fail to distinguish the trade of the head port of Boston from that of its members. For instance, none of the particular accounts which survive for Boston for eight years of Richard II's reign (1377–99) makes such a distinction.[14] When, however, these accounts do separate the trade of Boston itself from that of its member-ports, they again confirm that the trade of member-ports was on a minor scale. For instance, a particular account compiled by the Boston collectors for the year from March 1467 notes the arrival in Saltfleet Haven, a port to the north of Boston (see Map 1), of a ship called the 'Kateryn', of Veere (or 'Caumfer'), in Zeeland, on 27 April 1467 and again on 26 September 1467. The only goods on board were a variety of miscellaneous imports which were liable to the subsidy of poundage which was paid at the rate of 12d. in the pound (see section 2.9, below). In total, these imports made up less than 4% of the total value of miscellaneous denizen and non-Hanseatic alien goods for whose poundage the Boston collectors accounted during this year, quite apart from the wool, cloth, wine and Hanseatic goods which were liable to other duties which passed through head port.[15] It is likely, then, that the vast bulk of the trade for which the collectors of Boston's customs accounted was shipped through Boston itself.

The one period when a change in the geographical extent of the jurisdiction of the Boston customs collectors did have a significant impact on the figures for the port's trade contained in the customs account was in the two decades from 1353, when the Boston collectors were given control of the stretch of coastline which was normally administered from the head port of Lynn. As a result, their authority during this period extended as far as Blakeney, to the east of Lynn, which was usually the boundary between the Lynn and the Yarmouth customs administrations (see Map 1).[16] Unfortunately, neither the enrolled accounts nor the only surviving particular account for this period gives any indication of how trade was divided between Boston and Lynn during these years.[17] The significance of this merger of the Lynn and Boston customs jurisdictions for the apparent fluctuations in the individual branches of Boston's commerce is discussed below.

Naturally, it would be very convenient for the historian if the accounts produced by the medieval customs administration provided us with a reliable guide to the development of England's late medieval trade. Certainly, there do seem to have been a number of constraints on the collectors' dishonesty, including their supervision by controllers, the existence of searchers who had the responsibility to look for illegal

14 Rigby, *Overseas Trade of Boston*, p. xvi.

15 T.N.A., E122/10/8, ff. 13, 15v.

16 *Calendar of Fine Rolls, 1347–56*, p. 385; Carus-Wilson and Coleman, *England's Export Trade*, pp. 178, 182, 187–8, 190.

17 T.N.A., E122/7/10, for 1365–66, is the only surviving particular account for the period when the Lynn and Boston customs jurisdictions were merged.

trade, and regular Exchequer audits of the collectors' accounts, whilst the collectors themselves had a vested interest in being honest and efficient, since a third or more of the value of smuggled goods seized as forfeit went to the discoverer.[18] Nevertheless, there are reasons why we might question the reliability of the customs accounts as indicators of fluctuations in England's overseas trade in the later Middle Ages. For instance, Exchequer audits were of limited value, since the Exchequer could only audit the accounts which the customs officials themselves provided. The role of the controller as an independent control on the honesty of the collectors thus becomes a crucial issue. However, when we look at the periods for which we have accounts of both the controllers and collectors in Boston, their accounts seem remarkably similar, suggesting either that one account was based on the other, or that the two were drawn from a common source, probably that of a manifest provided by the shipmaster.[19] In itself, this certainly does not prove dishonesty on the part of the officials. After all, it could be argued that listing merchants in the same order in the two accounts facilitated a comparison between them and so allowed auditors to check more easily for any discrepancies. But it does mean that the surviving controllers' rolls were not independently compiled, which reduces their utility to historians as a check on the reliability of the collectors' returns.

Our faith in the reliability of the accounts produced by the customs collectors should be strengthened by the fact that there was a whole network of officials whose duties included the discovery of illegal trade. In Lincolnshire itself, the sheriff of the county, the bailiffs of Wainfleet, the mayor and bailiffs of Grimsby, and the bailiff and customs collectors of Boston all annually accounted for seizures of illegal imports and exports, as did the searchers for the Lindsey and Holland divisions of the county.[20] Yet, despite this comprehensive coverage, these officials reported, year after year, that they 'owed nothing' to the Exchequer.[21] They claimed that they had arrested nothing, even in periods when the Crown suspected that wool and other goods were being exported and imported without full payment of customs and subsidies,[22] that grain was being illegally shipped to Scotland from Lincolnshire ports,[23] and that cloth was being exported without paying customs, which resulted

18 Carus-Wilson and Coleman, *England's Export Trade*, pp. 23–4.

19 Rigby, *Overseas Trade of* Boston, pp. xxxii–iv. There was a similar resemblance between the returns of the collectors and the controller at Newcastle in 1499–1500 (*The Customs Accounts of Newcastle-upon-Tyne, 1454–1500*, ed. J. F. Wade (Surtees Society, 202 (1995)), p. 287).

20 See, for instance, T.N.A., Exchequer L.T.R. Memoranda Rolls, E368/153, Dies dati, Michaelmas, Hilary, Easter). For examples of the appointment of searchers for the jurisdiction of the Boston collectors, see *Calendar of Fine Rolls, 1391–99*, pp. 30, 60, 88, 191, 192.

21 See the accounts in T.N.A., E368/151 to E368/172.

22 *Calendar of Close Rolls, 1392–6*, p. 164.

23 T.N.A., E368/164, Recorda, Easter; *Calendar of Close Rolls, 1385–9*, p. 136. Of course, rumours of illegal trade did not always turn out to be true in particular cases (*Calendar of Close Rolls, 1381–5*, p. 417).

in the Boston collectors being required to swear in packers of cloth.[24] Thus, in the twenty-three years of Richard II's reign, the accounts of these Lincolnshire officials in the Lord Treasurer's Memoranda Rolls contain references to smuggling in only three years. Firstly, in 1378 the sheriff of Lincolnshire was ordered to distrain Richard Stightelbergh of Louth for £ 133 6s. 8d., which he owed for grain illegally taken from minor Lincolnshire ports to Scotland; Thomas Tinte owed £ 32 for the same offence at this time.[25] Secondly, in 1378–9, Philip Gernoun, the bailiff of Boston (and later himself a Boston customs collector), and the Boston customs collectors accounted for 45 woolfells worth 16s. 8d., which had been arrested in the ship of John Willard as uncustomed exports.[26] Finally, John Belle, the bailiff (and later customs collector) of Boston and the port's customs collectors accounted for £ 48 15s. of herring arrested as forfeit in December 1382.[27] These amounts are very minor indeed when compared with the total volume of trade passing through Boston at this time: in 1381–2, for instance, when £ 48 15s. of herring was arrested, over £ 12,000 of alien goods liable to the *ad valorem* custom of 3d. in the pound were imported and exported through Boston, quite apart from all of the other alien and denizen goods passing through the port. In fact, the Memoranda Roll accounts are not comprehensive in their record of seizures of illegal goods. Thus, whilst the account of the bailiff of Boston and the port's customs collectors for the year from Michaelmas 1385 reports that they owed nothing to the Exchequer for arrested goods, as they had found nothing that they could arrest, another account for the same period reveals that these men had actually seized four bales of madder which had been illegally imported and that they had then sold for £ 8 10s., a sum for which they had accounted at the Exchequer.[28] Even so, a total of £ 8 10s. of goods arrested in a year was insignificant when compared with the £ 6,942 of alien goods liable to the *ad valorem* duty of three pence in the pound, to which this madder was liable, during the same period.[29]

A similar impression arises from the accounts of the searchers who were supposed to uncover illegal imports and exports. Their accounts suggest that they

24 *Calendar of Fine Rolls, 1383–91*, p. 170. The Crown's order had no apparent effect on the amount of cloth exports returned in the customs accounts (Carus-Wilson and Coleman, *England's Export Trade*, p. 150). For complaints by Hanseatic merchants about the packers' failure to seal their cloth exports, see *Calendar of Close Rolls, 1385–9*, p. 220.

25 T.N.A., E368/151, Brevia retorna.

26 T.N.A., E368/152, Status et visus, Michaelmas. For Gernoun, see Rigby, *The Overseas Trade of Boston*, pp. 242–3.

27 P.R.O E368/156, Status et visus, Michaelmas; E122/7/16. For other references to smuggling in Lincolnshire, see T.N.A., E368/147, Recorda, Easter; Brevia retorna, Easter. For Belle, see Rigby, *Overseas Trade of Boston*, pp. 244–6.

28 T.N.A., E368/159, Dies dati, Michaelmas; E122/192/86.

29 T.N.A., E356/14.

rarely detected such illicit trade.[30] For instance, an account of Dennis de Lynn of Boston, searcher in the jurisdiction of the Boston customs collectors from Grimsby to Wisbech, survives for the four years from Easter 1412. In theory, Lynn was to have searched, or to have caused to have searched, all ships entering or leaving his jurisdiction which were suspected of carrying illegal cargoes. Yet, despite these wide powers, in this four-year period Lynn and his deputies arrested only five packs of woollen cloth, which had been exported uncustomed by a Boston merchant.[31] Similarly, in the fourteen-month period from November 1405, Lynn accounted for only £ 12 13s. 2d. of furs and osmund arrested as forfeit to the Crown.[32] It would seem that, in practice, the searchers discovered suspiciously little smuggling.

Carus-Wilson and Coleman argued that, in addition to the appointment of officials responsible for identifying smuggling, other factors worked to limit the extent of customs evasion in late medieval England. For instance, the Merchant Adventurers disapproved of smuggling whilst the Staple Company had a vested interest in preventing the illegal export of wool, the one commodity whose heavy rate of duty made it profitable to smuggle.[33] However, the Adventurers could hardly have been expected to condone in public the practice of illegal trading. Staple officials at Middelburg and Calais did help to regulate trade and did, on occasion, arrest small amounts of goods thought to be illegally shipped from Boston.[34] Nevertheless, these officials could only deal with trade that came to the staple, a destination which most smugglers probably preferred to avoid. In the fifteenth century, the Staple Company did have a financial interest in preventing smuggling, as from 1407 the Staplers made a series of loans to the Crown on the security of the customs revenues, whilst from 1466 they received customs revenues directly in return for their payment of the garrison at Calais. Before this time, however, the Staple Company was perhaps a less powerful force in the prevention of smuggling, although, of course, individual Staplers did have an interest in preventing their competitors from exporting wool without paying heavy duties, which would have allowed them to undercut those who traded legally.[35]

It is easy to see, then, why historians have sometimes raised doubts about the reliability of the accounts rendered by late medieval customs officials.[36] Certainly,

30 See, for instance, T.N.A., E122/189/151; E122/181/45; E122/131/38.

31 T.N.A., E122/181/45.

32 T.N.A., E122/131/38.

33 Carus-Wilson and Coleman, *England's Export Trade*, pp. 25–6.

34 T.N.A., Exchequer K.R. Memoranda Rolls, E159/170, Recorda, Easter; *Calendar of Close Rolls, 1385–9*, p. 31.

35 E. Power, 'The wool trade in the fifteenth century', in E. Power and M. M. Postan, eds, *Studies in English Trade in the Fifteenth Century* (London, 1935), pp.39–90, at 73–5.

36 See, for instance, an emphasis on the extent of smuggling and customs evasion in the fourteenth century in R. L. Baker, 'The English customs service, 1307–43: a study of medieval administration', *Transactions of the American Philosophical* Society, n.s., 51/6 (1961), pp. 3–76,

contemporaries themselves often questioned the honesty of the collectors. In 1390, for instance, parliament complained of the excessive favour shown by collectors towards merchants, a credible charge when it is remembered that, in ports such as Boston, the collectors were normally local merchants who were being asked to regulate the trade of their friends, neighbours, relatives and fellow guildsmen.[37] Moreover, in practice, it is unlikely that collectors always carried out their duties in person. For example, when William Spaigne died on 13 May 1385, not only was he a Boston customs collector, but also sheriff of Lincolnshire and an officer of the duchy of Lancaster.[38] In practice, much of the actual work of the customs collecting was probably done by a clerk employed by the collectors, who was paid out of the expenses which each pair of collectors was entitled to receive (amounting to £ 30 a year in the late fourteenth century).[39] The collectors themselves functioned chiefly as guarantors that the large sums of money paid for customs and subsidies would actually be handed over to the Crown or to those who had been granted assignments from the customs revenues. It is not surprising then that, as Stuart Jenks has shown, in those periods when royal officials were appointed as customs collectors and controllers, in place of local merchants, customs receipts went up, suggesting an improvement in the efficiency or honesty of the customs administration.[40]

Studies of particular periods in the history of the customs administration have challenged the reliability of the collectors' accounts. For example, it has been claimed that the shortcomings of the customs service in the years from 1336 to 1343 led to control of the customs administration being granted to a group of English merchants.[41] However, the rapid changes in royal policy in these years, when the Crown was attempting to finance the first phase of the Hundred Years' War, embargoes were being imposed on wool exports, and the unpopularity of royal fiscal policies among the merchant class was at its peak, meant that this was by no means a typical period for England's trade or for its customs administration. Similarly, whilst the introduction of outsiders and of royal clerks into the customs administrations

at 21; J. L. Blake, 'Medieval smuggling in the north-east: some fourteenth-century evidence', *Archaeologia Aeliana*, fourth series, 48 (1965), pp. 243–60, at 257; W. M. Ormrod, 'The English Crown and the customs', *Economic History Review*, 40 (1987), pp. 27–40, at 31–2; and N. Hybel, 'The grain trade in northern Europe before 1350', *Economic History Review*, 55 (2002), pp. 219–47, at 244.

37 *Rotuli Parliamentorum*, volume III, p. 281; C. Given-Wilson, ed., 'Richard II: parliament of November 1390, text and translation', item 27, in *The Parliament Rolls of Medieval England*, eds C. Given-Wilson et al., CD-ROM. Scholarly Digital Editions (Leicester, 2005).

38 T.N.A., E356/14; *Calendar of Fine Rolls, 1383–91*, p. 93; T.N.A., Duchy of Lancaster, Ministers' Accounts, DL29/242/3894. For Spaigne, see Rigby, *Overseas Trade of Boston*, pp. 225–9.

39 T.N.A., E356/14.

40 S. Jenks, 'Zollamt, Häfen und Außenhandel in England: ca. 1377–1470', *Vierteljahresschrift für Sozial- und Wirtschaftsgeschichte*, 75 (1988), pp. 305–38, at 335.

41 Baker, 'The English customs service, 1307–43', pp. 48–50.

of England's ports in the early 1390s, alongside the local merchants usually chosen as collectors, has sometimes been seen as a response to widespread corruption and dishonesty in the customs service, it is more likely that this change was actually the result of a desire to ensure the implementation of new royal policies concerning the location of the wool staple and the export of bullion.[42]

There were particular times when customs evasion may have been more prevalent, such as the late 1450s, a period of political conflict and administrative chaos in England during which the 'documentation of government activity in all spheres, including justice and finance, all but broke down'.[43] At Boston, for instance, there are no surviving enrolled customs accounts for the fifteenth months from Michaelmas 1458 to December 1459, a period which constitutes a rare break in the run of the port's enrolled customs returns in the later Middle Ages. There may also have been particular branches of trade, such as the export of tin, where the customs accounts are particularly untrustworthy, although tin exports were not normally shipped through Boston.[44] Overall, however, historians have tended to accept the general accuracy of the Exchequer customs accounts as evidence for the types of commodities and the volume of trade passing through England's ports.[45]

---

42 For this period, see A. Steel, 'The collectors of customs at Newcastle-upon-Tyne in the reign of Richard II', in J. Conway Davies, ed., *Studies Presented to Sir Hilary Jenkinson* (London, 1957), pp. 380–413; O. Coleman, 'The collectors of customs in London under Richard II', in A. E. J. Hollaender and W. Kellaway, eds, *Studies in London History* (London, 1969), pp. 181–94; A. Steel, 'The collectors of customs in the reign of Richard II', in H. Hearder and H. Loyn, eds, *British Government and Administration* (Cardiff, 1974), pp. 27–39; S. H. Rigby, 'The customs administration at Boston in the reign of Richard II', *Bulletin of the Institute of Historical Research*, 58 (1985), pp. 12–24; Rigby, *Overseas Trade of Boston*, pp. xxiii–xxx. For biographies of the men appointed as Boston collectors in this period, see Rigby, *Overseas Trade of Boston*, pp. 223–57 and S. H. Rigby, '"John of Gaunt's Palace" and the Sutton family of Lincoln', *Lincolnshire History and Archaeology*, 35 (2000), pp. 35–9.

43 J. Watts, *Henry VI and the Politics of Kingship* (Cambridge, 1996), p. 331; Carus-Wilson, *The Overseas Trade of Bristol*, p. 9.

44 J. Hatcher, *English Tin Production and Trade before 1500* (Oxford, 1973), pp. 110–16, 169. For tin and pewter exports through Boston, see the discussion of poundage in section 2.9, below. The late fifteenth-century Dartmouth customs returns for Exeter and Dartmouth may also understate the volume of cloth exports there (Oldland, *English Woollen Industry*, p. 280).

45 P. Ramsey, 'Overseas trade in the reign of Henry VII: the evidence of customs accounts', *Economic History Review*, second series, 6 (1953–4), pp. 173–182, at 173–7; Carus-Wilson and Coleman, *England's Export Trade*, pp. 18–33, 201–7; *Chester Customs Accounts, 1301–1566*, ed. K. P. Wilson (Record Society of Lancashire and Cheshire, 111 (1969)), p. 13; Childs, *The Customs Accounts of Hull*, pp. xiv–xviii; Cobb, *The Overseas Trade of London*, pp. xxviii–xxxiii; W. A. Harwood, 'The customs system in Southampton in the mid-fifteenth century', *Proceedings of the Hampshire Field Club and Archaeological Society*, 53 (1998), pp. 191–200, at 195–8; Rigby, *Overseas Trade of Boston*, pp. xxi–xxiii, xxx–xxxviii.

Perhaps the main reason for this acceptance of the basic reliability of the medieval customs accounts is that the rates of custom and subsidy levied on imports and exports were relatively low, meaning that there was little incentive to evade them by smuggling goods in or out of the country. For instance, in the late fifteenth century, when non-Hanseatic alien merchants imported or exported miscellaneous goods liable to the *ad valorem* custom introduced in 1303 and to the subsidy of poundage, they paid the custom at the rate of 3d. in the pound and the subsidy at the rate of 12d. in the pound, i.e. a combined rate of only 6.25 %; denizens, who did not pay the custom but were liable to poundage, were charged at the rate of only 5 %; Hansards, who were exempt from poundage at this time and so paid only the custom of 3d. in the pound, were liable at the even lower rate of 1.25 %. Moreover, the valuations of goods made for the purposes of levying these *ad valorem* duties were themselves rather low, being based on the prices at which merchants had originally bought the goods rather on than the price at which they sold them on, which further reduced the effective rate of custom being charged.[46] The customs and subsidies on England's cloth exports were also relatively low. For example, on the standard mid-fifteenth-century customs valuation of £ 1 15s. per broadcloth, Hanseatic merchants were paying a custom of 2.9 % per cloth exported, denizens were paying 3.3 % and non-Hanseatic alien merchants faced a combined custom and subsidy of 12.9 %.[47] Only for raw wool were customs and subsidies high enough (equivalent to around 25 % of its value for denizens and 33 % or more for aliens for most of our period) to make smuggling worthwhile; but wool was also one of the most bulky and difficult goods to conceal.[48] Given these low rates of custom and subsidy, even Jones, who presented smuggling as a 'key component' of Bristol's

---

46 *Calendar of Fine Rolls, 1461–71*, pp. 6–7; 274; Gras, *Early English Customs System*, pp. 263–4; Cobb, *Overseas Trade of London*, p. xxv; *The Customs Accounts of Hull, 1453–1490*, ed. W. R. Childs (Yorkshire Archaeological Society, Record Series, 144 (1986 for 1984)), pp. 16–18; S. Jenks, 'Capturing opportunity, financing trade', in W. Blockmans, M. M. Krom and J. Wubs-Mrozewicz, eds, *The Routledge Handbook of Maritime Trade Around Europe, 1300–1600* (London, 2017), pp. 36–56, at 37.

47 In this period, Hansards and denizens did not pay the subsidy of poundage on the value of their cloth exports (see section 2.9, below). If we add poundage, to which these merchants had been liable in the late fourteenth and early fifteenth centuries, Hanseatic cloths were being charged at 7.9 % and denizen cloths at 8.3 % (H. L. Gray, 'English foreign trade from 1446 to 1482', in Power and Postan, *Studies in English Trade in the Fifteenth Century*, pp. 1–38, 361–3, at 7). Since customs on cloth were levied per standard cloth and were at a fixed rate prior to 1558, their real rate fell even further as the weight and price of cloth rose in the late fifteenth century (J. Oldland, *The English Woollen Industry, c.1200–1560* (Abingdon, 2019), pp. 8, 202, 219, 277)

48 Carus-Wilson and Coleman, *England's Export Trade*, pp. 22–3; *The Overseas Trade of Bristol in the Later Middle Ages*, ed. E. M. Carus-Wilson (London, 1937), pp. 8–9; M. Bonney, 'The English medieval wool and cloth trade—new approaches for the local historian', *The Local*

trade in the sixteenth century, allowed that the incentives to trade illegally were 'fairly limited' in the years prior to *c.* 1530. Restrictions on exports of grain after 1516, on other foodstuffs from 1534 and on tanned hides after 1538 did increase the inducement to ship goods illegally and so, in the 1530s and 1540s, exports of leather and grain seem to have dominated Bristol's illicit trade. Illegal wine imports rose only from 1558, when there was an 18-fold increase in the level of duties, whilst smuggled cloth probably only accounted for a small proportion of total exports, even after 1558, when imposts on cloth exports were increased more than fivefold.[49]

As a result of their acceptance of the general reliability of the customs returns, historians have used the accounts as evidence for long-term changes in the volume and composition of England's commerce in this period, such as the shift from raw wool to manufactured woollen cloth in England's export trade, and the increasing monopolization of the country's overseas trade by London at the expense of the provincial ports.[50] Certainly, in the case of Boston itself, the fluctuations in the port's late medieval trade indicated by its customs accounts are so marked that they cannot be explained by short-term or marginal alterations in the reliability of the customs officials, but do seem to express genuine long-term changes in the scale and composition of the port's commerce.

Boston's particular and enrolled customs accounts have already been employed by a number of historians to establish some of the main trends in the port's trade in the later Middle Ages, or to examine specific aspects of its commerce, particularly the role of Hanseatic merchants.[51] Some of the information contained in the

Historian, 22/1 (1992), pp. 18–40, at 20–1; Wade, *Customs Accounts of Newcastle-upon-Tyne*, pp. 10–12; Oldland, *English Woollen Industry*, p. 194.

49 E. T. Jones, *Inside the Illicit Economy: Reconstructing the Smugglers' Trade of Sixteenth-Century Bristol* (Abingdon, 2016), pp. 33, 59, 103, 110, 185–6, 193–4, 197–203, 208–19, 223, 224–5; Oldland, *English Woollen Industry*, pp. 13, 245, 314.

50 On the shift from raw wool to cloth exports, see E. M. Carus-Wilson, *Medieval Merchant Venturers: Collected Studies* (second edition; London, 1967), pp. xviii–xxv; B. R. Mitchell, *British Historical Statistics* (Cambridge, 1988), pp. 358–9; S. Broadberry, B. M. S. Campbell, A. Klein, M. Overton, B. van Leeuwen, *British Economic Growth, 1270–1870* (Cambridge, 2015), 144–7; R. H. Britnell, *Britain and Ireland, 1050–1350: Economy and Society* (Cambridge, 2004), pp. 320–1, 326–31. For the growth of London, see the references in footnote 171, below.

51 For Boston's trade in this period, see W. I. Haward, 'The trade of Boston in the fifteenth century', *Associated Architectural Societies Reports and Papers*, 41 (1932–33), pp. 169–78; E. M. Carus-Wilson, 'The medieval trade of the ports of the Wash', *Medieval Archaeology*, 6–7 (1962–3), pp. 182–201; S. H. Rigby, 'Boston and Grimsby in the Middle Ages' (unpublished University of London Ph.D. thesis, 1983), chapters 4 and 7; S. H. Rigby, '"Sore decay" and "fair dwellings": Boston and urban decline in the later Middle Ages', *Midland History*, 10 (1985), pp. 47–61 at 49–55; and S. H. Rigby, 'Medieval Boston: economy, society and administration', in Badham and Cockerham, *'The beste and fayrest of al Lincolnshire'*, pp. 6–28. For the Hanse in Boston, see S. Jenks, *England, die Hanse und Preussen: Handel und Diplomatie*,

enrolled accounts has previously been tabulated for specific commodities, such as wool, cloth and wine,[52] or for particular periods, such as 1303–36,[53] 1399–1482,[54] and 1509–47.[55] The aim of this present study is to build on this previous work by bringing together in one place all of the statistical information contained in Boston's enrolled customs accounts for the years between 1279 and 1548, to explain how this information was originally compiled, and to outline the main changes which the port's trade underwent in this period.[56] The figures given here for Boston's trade between 1303 and 1548 are based on my own transcriptions of the enrolled customs accounts, which have been checked against those in Stuart Jenks's indispensable twelve volumes that calendar the enrolled accounts for all of England's ports in the years before 1512.[57] Statistics for exports of wool and hides for the years before 1303 (Figures 1.1 and 2.1) are drawn from Jenks's calendars of the enrolled customs

---

volumes I-III (Cologne, 1992); M. Burkhardt, 'One hundred years of thriving commerce at a major English sea port: the Hanseatic trade at Boston between 1370 and 1470', in H. Brand and L. Müller, eds, *The Dynamics of European Culture in the North Sea and Baltic Region* (Hilversum, 2007), pp. 65–85; J. D Fudge, *Cargoes, Embargoes and Emissaries: The Commercial and Political Interaction of England and the German Hanse, 1450–1510* (Toronto, 1995); P. M. Cawthorne, 'Medieval Boston and the German Hanse (*c.*1250–1474)', in B. Ayers, *et al.*, *Six Essays in Hanseatic History* (Cromer, 2017), pp. 26–52; and M. Burkhardt, 'The German Hanse and Bergen: new perspectives on an old subject', *Scandinavian Economic History Review*, 58 (2010), pp. 60–79, especially pp. 64–5. Pishey Thompson, the pioneering historian of Boston, made little use of the port's customs accounts since he was aware only of the enrolled accounts of the wool customs contained in the pipe rolls for 1279–1303 (P. Thompson, 'On the early commerce of Boston', *Associated Architectural Societies Reports and Papers*, 2 (1852–3), pp. 362–81, at 368–9; Thompson, *The History and Antiquities of Boston*, pp. 328–9).

52 Carus-Wilson and Coleman, *England's Export Trade*, pp. 36–119; A. Beardwood, *Alien Merchants in England, 1350 to 1377: Their Legal and Economic Position* (Cambridge, Mass., 1931), pp. 145, 165–6, 178–80; M. K. James, *Studies in the Medieval Wine Trade*, ed. E. M. Veale (Oxford, 1971), pp. 96–116.

53 T. H. Lloyd, *Alien Merchants in England in the High Middle Ages* (Brighton, 1982), Table A, I.6.

54 H. L. Gray, 'Tables of enrolled customs and subsidy accounts: 1399–1482', in Power and Postan, *Studies in English Trade in the Fifteenth Century*, pp. 321–60, at 330–33. For other studies giving information from the enrolled accounts, see Carus-Wilson and Coleman, *England's Export Trade*, pp. 4–6.

55 G. Schanz, *Englische Handelspolitik gegen Ende des Mittelalters mit besonderer Berücksichtigung des Zeitalters der beiden ersten Tudors Heinrich VII und Heinrich VIII* (two volumes, Leipzig, 1881), II: 57, 71, 77, 101, 115, 125, 145, 154.

56 The figures given below supplement, correct and supersede those provided in Rigby, 'Boston and Grimsby in the Middle Ages', pp. 454–83.

57 Jenks, *The Enrolled Customs Accounts, Parts 1–12*. The notes to the tables below note my rare disagreements with Dr Jenks's astonishingly accurate transcriptions of the figures in Boston's enrolled accounts.

accounts contained in the Exchequer pipe rolls.[58] In both the tables and the graphs below, figures for twelve-month periods are given wherever possible, but the accounting periods used in the enrolled accounts sometimes mean that totals are for more or less than a full year. In the graphs, no attempt has been made to adjust or estimate figures so that they form an estimate of the volume of trade within twelve-month periods, as Carus-Wilson and Coleman did in their graphs of wool and cloth exports.[59] In those cases when the customs returns cover more or less than an entire year, care should be taken when using the tables and graphs below as indications of short-term fluctuations in Boston's trade.

58 Jenks, *Enrolled Customs Accounts*, Part 1. See also Carus-Wilson and Coleman, *England's Export Trade*, pp. 36–40.

59 Carus-Wilson and Coleman, *England's Export Trade*, pp. 10–11, 16, 18.

2.
Boston's overseas trade, 1279–1548

2.1 Wool exports, 1279–1548

The levies imposed by the Crown on wool exports allow us to follow the changing fortunes of England's wool trade in the later Middle Ages. The first duty on wool exports was introduced in 1275, when Edward I imposed a custom (i.e. a permanent levy at a fixed rate) on exports of wool and woolfells which was paid by both denizen and alien merchants at the rate of at 6s. 8d. per sack of wool (i.e. 364 lbs) or per 300 woolfells.[60] From 1368, the rate of custom was increased to 6s. 8d. per 240 woolfells and so, in order to compare the volume of wool exported before and after this date, we need to convert exports of woolfells into their equivalent as sacks of wool at a consistent rate throughout the entire period; it is this post-1368 figure which is used in Figures 1.1 and 1.2 below.[61] However, since woolfells made up only a small part of this trade when Boston's wool exports were at their peak, the choice of whether to use a figure of 240 or 300 fells per sack of wool has little impact on the long-term trends revealed in the table and graph below. Woolfells did make up a higher proportion of wool exports in the early sixteenth century, but by then the total volume of this trade was much reduced from its fourteenth-century heyday.

In 1303, Edward I granted a charter of liberties, the *Carta Mercatoria*, to foreign merchants, who, in return, agreed to pay various additional customs to the Crown.[62] These new duties included an extra 3s. 4d. per sack of wool or 300 woolfells exported (changed to 240 fells from 1368, as noted above), which henceforth allows us to distinguish wool exports by denizen merchants from those made by aliens, whether Hansards or non-Hanseatic aliens.[63] From 1303, the 1275 custom became known as the 'ancient custom', in contrast with the 'new custom' of 1303, whilst the ancient custom of 1275 and the 1303 new custom on wool, woolfells and hides together eventually became known as the 'great custom'.[64]

Although we do not have returns for wool exports for the very earliest years of the wool custom, accounts do survive from 1279 onwards, when they were included in the Exchequer pipe rolls (although the accounts for 1291 to 1294 are missing),

---

60 Gras, *Early English Customs System*, p. 223; Jenks, *Enrolled Customs Accounts*, Part 3, p. iv.

61 Carus-Wilson and Coleman, *England's Export Trade*, p. 13; Jenks, *Enrolled Customs Accounts*, Part 1, p. vi.

62 S. Jenks, 'Die Carta Mercatoria. Ein hansisches Privileg', *Hansische Geschichtsblätter*, 108, (1990), pp. 45–86.

63 Gras, *Early English Customs System*, pp. 66, 262; Jenks, *Enrolled Customs Accounts*, Part 3, p.v.

64 Gras, *Early English Customs System*, pp. 60–1, 74–5.

and then, from 1303, were recorded in separate rolls.[65] There are occasional gaps in the series of Boston returns. For instance, from 30 January 1333 to 6 June 1334, when there was a home staple at Lincoln, returns for the customs on wool (as well as on the other staple goods of hides and lead) were made by customs officials based in that city rather than in Boston, although customs on non-staple goods, such as cloth and wax, continued to be collected at Boston. The period covered by the returns for the wool custom at Boston, i.e. up to 2 February 1333 and from 24 May 1334, slightly overlap with those when it was being collected at Lincoln.[66] The totals in Figure 1.1 thus include all the wool on which custom was paid in Boston and Lincoln during these two years. A more significant gap in the returns for the duties introduced in 1275 is that from 1343 to 1351, when the customs for all ports were farmed by a consortium of English merchants, which means that we do not have annual returns of the custom from individual ports.[67] The new custom of 1303 was not paid during two brief periods: from August 1309 to August 1310, when it was temporarily stopped, and from October 1311 to July 1322, when it was again abolished as part of the Ordainers' reform of Edward II's finances.[68] The new custom was also included in the grant of the customs to the consortium of English merchants from 1343 to 1351 (see above), which means that we lack figures for it during these years. As noted above, the merger of the Lynn and Boston customs jurisdiction for twenty years after 1353 complicates the interpretation of the customs figures. However, since wool exports at Lynn, both before and after this period, were of minor significance compared to those at Boston, it seems likely that the bulk of the wool exports for which the Boston customs collectors accounted in the two decades from 1353 was shipped through Boston itself.

In addition to its permanent customs revenues, the Crown also benefitted from the levying of a subsidy on wool exports, i.e. a duty which was granted at a variable rate for some specific term, such as a number of years or for the life of the king.[69] From the start of the Hundred Years' War, these subsidies became a regular imposition and were levied at much higher rates than the 1275 and 1303 customs. In Edward III's reign, the subsidy was usually charged at between 33s. 4d and 43s. 4d. per sack of wool exported, compared with only 6s. 8d. per sack which denizens paid for the ancient custom and 10s. per sack paid by aliens for the ancient custom and new custom.[70] Similarly, for most of the fifteenth century, denizen merchants paid

65 Carus-Wilson and Coleman, *England's Export Trade*, pp. 157–8.

66 T. H. Lloyd, *The English Wool Trade in the Middle Ages* (Cambridge, 1977), p. 121; T.N.A., E356/4, m. 15; E356/8, m. 25; E356/10, mm. 15, 16d.

67 E. B. Fryde, *Studies in Medieval Trade and Finance* (London, 1983), chapter 10.

68 Lloyd, *Alien Merchants in England*, pp. 30–1.

69 Gras, *Early English Customs System*, pp. 77–80.

70 W. M. Ormrod, *The Reign of Edward III: Crown and Political Society, 1327–1377* (London, 1990), p. 206.

40s. subsidy per sack of wool exported; aliens paid the subsidy at an even higher rate which, in 1471, was fixed at 76s. 8d. per sack.[71] The returns of subsidies levied in 1347–48 and 1350–1 usefully reveal the level of wool exports during the period when we do not have figures for the ancient and new customs because they were at farm.[72]

Figures 1.1 and 1.2 below give the total of wool sacks exported from Boston between 1279 and 1548, with woolfells converted to sacks of wool at the rate of 240 fells per sack, and with totals rounded up or down to the nearest sack.[73] When the accounts begin, in the decade from 1279, Boston was England's pre-eminent port for the shipment of wool at a time when raw wool was by far the country's main export commodity; over 9,000 sacks a year were sent through the port in this period, around a third of the national total.[74] Boston fair, which began on St Botolph's day (17 June), was one of England's leading fairs at a time when the country's wholesale trade was based on a succession of such marts, and it was the main fair at which wool was sold, or was at least delivered to merchants by producers.[75] Boston drew mainly on the wool of the Welsh borders and Midlands, from Flintshire, Cheshire, Staffordshire and Shropshire through Leicestershire, Derbyshire, Northamptonshire, Rutland, Warwickshire and Nottinghamshire, as well as on the fine-quality wool of Lincolnshire itself.[76] The trade in Boston reached its peak in the years after 1304, when England's wool output was recovering after a series of sheep murrains.[77] Over 10,000 sacks of wool a year were exported there during this period, representing the wool of almost two and a half million sheep, with over half of this wool being shipped by alien merchants, including Italians from Florence, Lucca and Piacenza. However, by this date, Boston had been overtaken by London, where denizen merchants dominated the trade, as the leading export port for wool, although Boston did briefly regain its primacy in the early 1330s, when alien trade in the capital was suffering a decline.[78]

---

71 Carus-Wilson and Coleman, *England's Export Trade*, p. 194.

72 T.N.A., E356/5, mm. 10, 11, 12, 13d., 14; E356/12, mm. 2d., 3, 5, 6d. Carus-Wilson and Coleman, *England's Export Trade*, p. 46 omits the figure for 1347–8.

73 Some of these figures differ from those given by Carus-Wilson and Coleman in *England's Export Trade*, but such differences are usually slight and generally result from the ways in which totals have been rounded up or down to the nearest sack. Significant differences with their figures are given in the notes to Figure 1.1.

74 Figures for wool exports nationally and for ports other than Boston are taken from Carus-Wilson and Coleman, *England's Export Trade*, pp. 36–74, 122–3.

75 A. R. Bell, C. Brooks and P. R. Dryburgh, *The English Wool Market, c. 1230–1327* (Cambridge, 2007), pp. 56–8. For the history of the fair, see Rigby, *Boston, 1086–1225*, pp. 41–8, 67; Rigby, 'Medieval Boston', pp. 9–12.

76 For references, see Rigby, 'Medieval Boston', pp. 9–11.

77 P. Slavin, 'Mites and merchants: the crisis of English wool and textiles revisited', *Economic History Review*, 73 (2020), pp. 885–913, at 887–97.

78 Lloyd, *Alien Merchants in England*, p. 52; Rigby, 'Boston and Grimsby in the Middle Ages', pp. 173–77.

As is well known, the long-term fortunes of England's wool trade in the fourteenth and fifteenth centuries were determined by changes in government policy, which included the imposition of heavy duties on wool exports, the choice of home or foreign ports as staples through which the wool trade was funnelled, and the introduction of bullion and credit regulations.[79] As a result of these policies, by the end of the fourteenth century the composition of Boston's wool trade was very different from that of a hundred years earlier, with total exports having fallen by around two thirds, in line with the national trend. In the early 1350s, a monopoly of English wool exports had been granted to alien merchants, but by the end of the century alien exports at Boston had been reduced to a trickle, as the Crown had come to favour a monopoly company of English merchants who shipped their wool to the staple at Calais, with Italian wool exports now being channelled through Southampton. In the fifteenth century, alien exports at Boston disappeared, which meant that, in effect, denizen exports became the equivalent of total exports (as in Figure 1.2). By the end of the fifteenth century, the port's wool exports had fallen by a further half, and this decline continued thereafter until, by the 1540s, an average of fewer than 400 sacks of wool a year passed through it, a far cry from the 10,000 or more which had once been shipped. What remained of England's wool exports was increasingly sent from London.[80]

Figure 1.1 Wool exports from Boston, 1279–1548 (sacks).

	Denizen	Alien	Total	
19.5.1279–19.5.1280			7699	
19.5.1280–13.4.1281			10196	
13.4.1281–29.3.1282			10793	
29.3.1282–18.4.1283			9337	
18.4.1283–9.4.1284			11208	
9.4.1284–25.3.1285			9662	
25.3.1285–14.4.1286			8823	
14.4.1286–6.4.1287			9117	

79 On the wool trade, see E. E. Power, 'The wool trade in the fifteenth century', in Power and Postan, *Studies in English Trade in the Fifteenth Century*, pp. 39–90; E. Power, *The Wool Trade in Medieval English History* (Oxford, 1941); Lloyd, *The English Wool Trade in the Middle Ages*; J. H. Munro, *Wool, Cloth and Gold: The Struggle for Bullion in Anglo-Burgundian Trade, 1340–1478* (Toronto, 1972); S. Rose, *The Wealth of England: The Wool Trade and its Political Importance, 1100–1600* (Oxford, 2017); Oldland, *English Woollen Industry*, pp. 15, 194–5.

80 For references, see Rigby, 'Medieval Boston', pp. 10–11, 14–17, 23. See also Oldland, *English Woollen Industry*, p. 262.

	Denizen	Alien	Total	
6.4.1287–28.3.1288			9373	
28.3.1288–10.4.1289			9585	
10.4.1289–2.4.1290			10061	
2.4.1290–22.4.1291			10383	Note 1
22.4.1291–29.7.1294	No returns			
29.7.1294–Mich.1295			6054	
Mich.1295–Mich.1296			3972	
Mich.1296–Mich.1297			5838	
Mich.1297–7.5.1298			1826	
7.5.1298–7.6.1299	No returns			
7.6.1299–Mich.1299			3858	
Mich.1299–Mich.1300			8268	
Mich.1300–Mich.1301			9958	
Mich.1301–Mich.1302			4472	
Mich.1302–30.9.1303		2247	7561	Note 2
30.9.1303–Mich.1304	2513	2703	5216	
Mich.1304–Mich.1305	3561	7477	11038	
Mich.1305–Mich.1306	3636	5370	9006	
Mich.1306–Mich.1307	3816	6394	10210	
Mich.1307–Mich.1308	4254	5344	9598	
Mich.1308–Mich.1309	5209	5883	11092	
Mich.1309–Mich.1310	4683	5045	9728	
Mich.1310–Mich.1311	4678	5125	9803	
Mich.1311–Mich.1312			11191	Note 3
Mich.1312–Mich.1313			10396	
Mich.1313–Mich.1314			8566	
Mich.1314–Mich.1315			7269	
Mich.1315–Mich.1316			5759	
Mich.1316–Mich.1317			6552	
Mich.1317–Mich.1318			5627	
Mich.1318–Mich.1319			4277	
Mich.1319–Mich.1320			5477	
Mich.1320–Mich–1321			4838	
Mich.1321–Mich.1322			2241	Note 4
Mich.1322–Mich.1323	1841	5139	6980	
Mich.1323–Mich.1324	1748	3267	5015	
Mich.1324–Mich.1325	1410	3410	4820	
Mich.1325–Mich.1326	690	1967	2657	
Mich.1326–Mich.1327	2139	3033	5172	

	Denizen	Alien	Total	
Mich.1327–27.8.1328	2690	2045	4735	
27.8.1328–Mich.1329	3615	4045	7660	
Mich.1329–Mich.1330	2306	3561	5867	Note 5
Mich.1330–Mich.1331	2523	3356	5879	Note 6
Mich.1331–Mich.1332	2396	4083	6479	
Mich.1332–Mich.1333	2395	4043	6438	Note 7
Mich.1333–Mich.1334	4376	3290	7666	Note 8
Mich.1334–Mich.1335	3431	3487	6918	
Mich.1335–Mich.1336	2662	2551	5213	
Mich.1336–Mich.1337	0	0	0	
Mich.1337–Mich.1338	2596	2377	4973	
Mich.1338–24.4.1340	5616	5328	10944	Note 9
24.4.1340–22.2.1341	666	1825	2491	Note 10
22.2.1341–Mich.1341	1458	1175	2633	Note 11
Mich.1341–16.6.1342	3191	862	4053	Note 12
16.6.1342–15.7.1343	1493	2122	3615	Note 13
15.7.1343–15.3.1347	No returns			
15.3.1347–20.4.1348			4096	Note 14
20.4.1348–24.9.1350	No returns			
24.9.1350–Mich.1351			5438	
Mich.1351–3.9.1352	2181	448	2629	
3.9.1352–Mich.1353	0	3438	3438	
Mich.1353–Mich.1354	0	7433	7433	
Mich.1354–Mich.1355	0	6049	6049	
Mich.1355–Mich.1356	0	4020	4020	
Mich.1356–30.9.1357			6521	Note 15
30.9.1357–Mich.1358			5112	
Mich.1358–Mich.1359			5072	
Mich.1359–Mich.1360			6424	
Mich.1360–Mich.1361			5437	
Mich.1361–Mich.1362			9163	
Mich.1362–Mich.1363	1676	2007	3638	
Mich.1363–2.10.1364	2260	1635	3895	Note 16
2.10.1364–20.10.1365	3259	2562	5821	
20.10.1365–Mich.1366	4117	1585	5702	
Mich.1366–Mich.1367	3564	1769	5333	
Mich.1367–Mich.1368	4009	961	4970	
Mich.1368–Mich.1369	2550	4716	7266	
Mich.1369–Mich.1370	0	3212	3212	

	Denizen	Alien	Total	
Mich.1370–Mich.1371	4201	1825	6026	
Mich.1371–Mich.1372			4286	
Mich.1372–Mich.1373	2732	4644	7376	
Mich.1373–Mich.1374	2460	2783	5243	
Mich.1374–Mich.1375	3313	4183	7496	
Mich.1375–Mich.1376	3439	2301	5740	
Mich.1376–26.8.1377	2949	336	3285	
26.8.1377–Mich.1378	5058	446	5504	Note 17
Mich.1378–Mich.1379	2593	7	2600	
Mich.1379–Mich.1380	3843	128	3971	
Mich.1380–Mich.1381	3304	204	3508	
Mich.1381–Mich.1382	2813	674	3487	
Mich.1382–Mich.1383	2462	650	3112	
Mich.1383–Mich.1384	3733	411	4144	
Mich.1384–Mich.1385	2082	414	2496	
Mich.1385–Mich.1386	2271	387	2658	
Mich.1386–26.11.1387	4390	510	4900	
26.11.1387–Mich.1388	2362	127	2489	Note 18
Mich.1388–Mich.1389	3074	197	3271	Note 19
Mich.1389–Mich.1390	4211	240	4451	
Mich.1390–Mich.1391	2463	528	2991	
Mich.1391–Mich.1392	3287	1230	4517	Note 20
Mich.1392–Mich.1393	3740	176	3916	
Mich.1393–Mich.1394	3133	134	3267	
Mich.1394–Mich.1395	2641	233	2874	
Mich.1395–Mich.1396	2990	129	3119	
Mich.1396–Mich.1397	3405	104	3509	Note 21
Mich.1397–Mich.1398	3149	99	3248	Note 22
Mich.1398–Mich.1399	3313	9	3322	
Mich.1399–Mich.1400	3072	0	3072	
Mich.1400–2.10.1401	3006	0	3006	
2.10.1401–2.10.1402	3018	0	3018	
2.10.1402–Mich.1403	1030	0	1030	
Mich.1403–Mich.1404	1506	0	1506	
Mich.1404–Mich.1405	2746	0	2746	
Mich.1405–3.10.1406	2109	0	2109	
3.10.1406–Mich.1407	2201	0	2201	
Mich.1407–Mich.1408	1945	0	1945	
Mich.1408–Mich.1409	2881	19	2900	

	Denizen	Alien	Total	
Mich.1409–Mich.1410	2169	0	2169	
Mich.1410–Mich.1411	1749	0	1749	
Mich.1411–Mich.1412	2585	0	2585	
Mich.1412–Mich.1413	2597	0	2597	
Mich.1413–Mich.1414	1944	0	1944	
Mich.1414–Mich.1415	2555	0	2555	
Mich.1415–Mich.1416	2020	0	2020	
Mich.1416–Mich.1417	2382	0	2382	
Mich.1417–Mich.1418	2637	0	2637	
Mich.1418–Mich.1419	2236	0	2236	
Mich.1419–10.10.1420	2098	0	2098	
10.10.1420–Mich.1421	1705	0	1705	
Mich.1421–31.8.1422	1985	0	1985	
1.9.1422–Mich.1423	1821	0	1821	
Mich.1423–Mich.1424	1897	0	1897	
Mich.1424–Mich.1425	2031	0	2031	
Mich.1425–Mich.1426	2436	0	2436	
Mich.1426–Mich.1427	3714	0	3714	
Mich.1427–Mich.1428	2673	0	2673	
Mich.1428–1.11.1429	2566	0	2566	
1.11.1429–1.11.1430	894	0	894	
1.11.1430–20.10.1431	1693	0	1693	
20.10.1431–Mich.1432	1468	0	1468	
Mich.1432–Mich.1433	1910	0	1910	
Mich.1433–Mich.1434	0	0	0	
Mich.1434–Mich.1435	3157	0	3157	
Mich.1435–10.10.1436	0	0	0	
10.10.1436–11.11.1437	0	0	0	
11.11.1437–Mich.1438	0	0	0	
Mich.1438–Mich.1439	0	0	0	
Mich.1439–Mich.1440	3893	0	3893	
Mich.1440–30.6.1441	1049	0	1049	
30.6.1441–Mich.1442	0	0	0	
Mich.1442–12.8.1443	2855	0	2855	
12.8.1443–12.10.1444	2484	0	2484	
12.10.1444–12.10.1445	0	0	0	
12.10.1445–24.6.1446	3593	0	3593	
24.6.1446–18.7.1447	17	0	17	
18.7.1447–21.11.1448	2291	2	2293	

	Denizen	Alien	Total	
21.11.1448–21.11.1449	0	0	0	
21.11.1449–Mich.1450	4565	0	4565	
Mich.1450–3.2.1452	1100	0	1100	
3.2.1452–Mich.1452	2776	0	2776	
Mich.1452–Mich.1453	0	0	0	
Mich.1453–Mich.1454	61	0	61	
Mich.1454–10.10.1455	5237	0	5237	
10.10.1455–10.10.1456	0	0	0	
10.10.1456–Mich.1457	0	0	0	
Mich.1457–Mich.1458	2364	0	2364	
Mich.1458–15.12.1459	No returns			
15.12.1459–1.9.1460	0	0	0	
1.9.1460–Mich.1461	2771	0	2771	
Mich.1461–Mich.1462	54	0	54	
Mich.1462–20.7.1463	1116	0	1116	
20.7.1463–25.2.1465	1102	0	1102	
25.2.1465–Mich.1465	2165	0	2165	
Mich.1465–25.3.1467	2132	0	2132	
25.3.1467–6.3.1468	1949	0	1949	
6.3.1468–25.12.1468	153	0	153	
25.12.1468–Mich.1469	2437	0	2437	
Mich.1469–13.11.1470	1950	0	1950	Note 23
26.10.1470–Mich.1471	22	0	22	Note 24
Mich.1471–8.10.1472	3655	0	3655	
8.10.1472–8.10.1473	1535	0	1535	
8.10.1473–6.4.1474	1068	0	1068	
6.4.1474–Mich.1475	1372	0	1372	
Mich.1475–Mich.1476	2220	0	2220	
Mich.1476–Mich.1477	0	0	0	
Mich.1477–Mich.1478	2291	0	2291	
Mich.1478–Mich.1479	1378	0	1378	
Mich.1479–Mich.1480	1226	0	1226	
Mich.1480–Mich.1481	1606	0	1606	
Mich.1481–Mich.1482	1515	0	1515	
Mich.1482–Mich.1483	989	0	989	
Mich.1483–Mich.1484	778	0	778	
Mich.1484–Mich.1485	883	0	883	
Mich.1485–Mich.1486	1394	0	1394	
Mich.1486–Mich.1487	1525	0	1525	

	Denizen	Alien	Total	
Mich.1487–Mich.1488	2010	0	2010	
Mich.1488–Mich.1489	1072	0	1072	
Mich.1489–Mich.1490	2338	0	2338	
Mich.1490–Mich.1491	0	0	0	
Mich.1491–Mich.1492	0	0	0	
Mich.1492–Mich.1493	1478	0	1478	
Mich.1493–Mich.1494	867	0	867	
Mich.1494–Mich.1495	1337	0	1337	
Mich.1495–Mich.1496	2026	0	2026	
Mich.1496–Mich.1497	956	0	956	
Mich.1497–Mich.1498	1444	0	1444	
Mich.1498–Mich.1499–	1041	0	1041	
Mich.1499–Mich.1500	190	0	190	
Mich.1500–Mich.1501	1524	0	1524	
Mich.1501–Mich.1502	1702	0	1702	
Mich.1502–Mich.1503	2209	0	2209	
Mich.1503–Mich.1504	628	0	628	
Mich.1504–Mich.1505	1489	0	1489	
Mich.1505–Mich.1506	657	0	657	
Mich.1506–Mich.1507	1151	0	1151	
Mich.1507–Mich.1508	1120	0	1120	
Mich.1508–Mich.1509	1066	0	1066	
Mich.1509–Mich.1510	1332	0	1332	
Mich.1510–Mich.1511	1165	0	1165	
Mich.1511–Mich.1512	1101	0	1101	
Mich.1512–Mich.1513	530	0	530	
Mich.1513–Mich.1514	976	0	976	
Mich.1514–Mich.1515	1220	0	1220	
Mich.1515–Mich.1516	1136	0	1136	
Mich.1516–Mich.1517	1162	0	1162	
Mich.1517–Mich.1518	1316	0	1316	
Mich.1518–Mich.1519	1377	0	1377	
Mich.1519–Mich.1520	1185	0	1185	
Mich.1520–Mich.1521	1071	0	1071	
Mich.1521–Mich.1522	742	0	742	
Mich.1522–Mich.1523	483	0	483	
Mich.1523–Mich.1524	278	0	278	
Mich.1524–Mich.1525	271	0	271	
Mich.1525–Mich.1526	249	0	249	

	Denizen	Alien	Total	
Mich.1526–Mich.1527	509	0	509	
Mich.1527–Mich.1528	389	0	389	
Mich.1528–Mich.1529	280	0	280	
Mich.1529–Mich.1530	292	0	292	
Mich.1530–Mich.1531	148	0	148	
Mich.1531–Mich.1532	187	0	187	
Mich.1532–Mich.1533	0	0	0	
Mich.1533–Mich.1534	358	0	358	
Mich.1534–Mich.1535	399	0	399	
Mich.1535–Mich.1536	513	0	513	
Mich.1536–Mich.1537	799	0	799	
Mich.1537–Mich.1538	392	0	392	
Mich.1538–Mich.1539	588	0	588	
Mich.1539–Mich.1540	697	0	697	
Mich.1540–Mich.1541	634	0	634	
Mich.1541–Mich.1542	961	0	961	
Mich.1542–Mich.1543	0	0	0	
Mich.1543–Mich.1544	633	0	633	
Mich.1544–Mich.1545	0	0	0	
Mich.1545–Mich.1546	237	0	237	
Mich.1546–Mich.1547	70	0	70	
Mich.1547–Mich.1548	0	0	0	

(Sources: 1279–1303: Jenks, The Enrolled Customs Accounts, Part I; Carus-Wilson and Coleman, England's Export Trade, pp. 36–40.[81] *1303–1548: T.N.A., E356 Enrolled customs accounts)*

Notes to Figure 1.1:

- Note 1. The figure for 1290–91 comes from Carus-Wilson and Coleman, *England's Export Trade,* p. 38, which is drawn from T.N.A., E122/5/2.
- Note 2. Alien exports are distinguished as such from 10 February 1303.
- Note 3. The total for this year includes 647 sacks exported by aliens before 27 October 1311, when the new customs was abolished by the Ordainers (T.N.A., E356/2, m. 29).
- Note 4. The total for this year includes 491 sacks exported by aliens from 20 July to Michaelmas 1322 (T.N.A., E356/2, m. 46).
- Note 5. Carus-Wilson and Coleman, *England's Export Trade*, p. 44 lists the total for alien wool exports paying the new custom (T.N.A., E356/10, m. 16) in

81 For details of the works cited in the notes to the Figures, see the bibliography, below.

the column for denizen exports for this year, and gives the denizen total in the column for alien exports.

- Note 6. Carus-Wilson and Coleman, *England's Export Trade*, p. 44 gives a total of 5,860 sacks exported for this year.
- Note 7. The total includes 3,499 sacks customed in Lincoln.
- Note 8. The total includes 3,900 sacks customed in Lincoln.
- Note 9. 1338–40: Carus-Wilson and Coleman, *England's Export Trade*, p. 45 gives a total of 5,799 sacks of denizen wool exported in this period.
- Note 10. Carus-Wilson and Coleman, *England's Export Trade*, p. 46 does not give separate figures for denizen and alien wool in this period.
- Note 11. Carus-Wilson and Coleman, *England's Export Trade*, p. 46 gives a total of 2,693 sacks exported for this period, made up of 1,165 denizen and 1,528 alien sacks of wool
- Note 12. Carus-Wilson and Coleman, *England's Export Trade*, p. 46 does not distinguish denizen and alien exports in this period.
- Note 13. Carus-Wilson and Coleman, *England's Export Trade*, p. 46 does not distinguish denizens and aliens in this period, and gives a total of 3,479 sacks exported.
- Note 14. Carus-Wilson and Coleman, *England's Export Trade*, p. 46 omits the figure for 1347–8, which can be calculated from the subsidy returns for this year (T.N.A., E356/5, mm. 10, 11, 12).
- Note 15. From 1356 to 1362, denizen and alien rates of custom cannot be distinguished in the enrolled accounts, as denizens paid the higher alien rate of custom with the new custom accounts giving wool exports as being by '*diversi mercatores*' (Carus-Wilson and Coleman, *England's Export Trade*, p. 48; Lloyd, *The English Wool Trade in the Middle Ages*, pp. 208, 214; Beardwood, *Alien Merchants in England*, p. 26; T.N.A., E356/8, mm. 24–24d.)
- Note 16. The total excludes 53 sarplars of wool, for which no equivalent in sacks is given in the enrolled account, which were lost at sea after being exported (T.N.A., E356/5, m. 19).
- Note 17. Carus-Wilson and Coleman, *England's Export Trade*, p. 51 gives 5,781 denizen sacks exported.
- Note 18. Carus-Wilson and Coleman, *England's Export Trade*, p. 52 gives 2,366 denizen and 125 alien sacks exported.
- Note 19. Carus-Wilson and Coleman, *England's Export Trade*, p. 52 gives 2,736 denizen and 192 alien sacks exported.
- Note 20. Carus-Wilson and Coleman, *England's Export Trade*, p. 53 gives 3,277 denizen and 1,182 alien sacks exported.
- Note 21. The enrolled account for Michaelmas 1396 to Michaelmas 1397 includes the custom and subsidy paid on 3,302½ and 3 cloves of wool exported by denizen merchants (T.N.A., E356/14, m. 15); this is given as 3,212½ sacks and 3 cloves in Jenks, *Enrolled Customs Accounts*, Part 5, p. 1194.

- Note 22. Carus-Wilson and Coleman, *England's Export Trade*, p. 54 gives 140 alien sacks exported.
- Note 23. Dates as given in the enrolled account (T.N.A., E356/21, m. 30).
- Note 24. Dates as given in the enrolled account (T.N.A., E356/21, m. 30).

Figure 1.2 Wool exports from Boston, 1279–1548 (sacks)

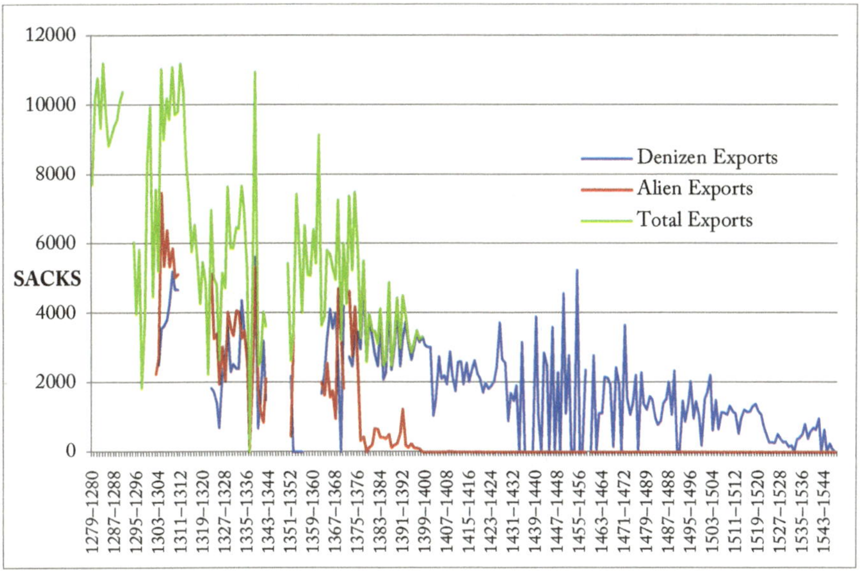

2.2 Hide exports, 1279–1548

The custom on wool introduced in 1275 was accompanied by a custom on cow hides, which was charged at the rate of 13s. 4d. per last of hides (a last consisted of 20 dickers, i.e. 200 hides).[82] The 1303 new custom imposed an extra 6s. 8d. per last of hides exported by alien merchants, whether they were Hansards or other aliens, which henceforth allows us to distinguish denizen and alien exports.[83] This new custom was not levied in 1309–10 and 1311–22, and no returns for either custom exist from 1343 to 1351 (as above), although a subsidy on hides does provide a total for 1350–51. The particular and enrolled accounts usually refer to these goods simply as 'hides', but they are sometimes specified as being hides with the hair

82 Gras, *Early English Customs System*, pp. 223–4; Jenks, *Enrolled Customs Accounts*, Part 3, p. iv.

83 Gras, *Early English Customs System*, pp. 66, 262–3; Jenks, *Enrolled Customs Accounts*, Part 3, p.v.

still attached,[84] tanned hides,[85] ox-hides,[86] tanned ox-hides,[87] salted ox-hides[88] or calf-skins.[89]

Figures 2.1 and 2.2 give the totals of hides exported from Boston from 1279 measured in lasts, dickers and hides. The trade there was at its peak in the 1280s, with around 16½ lasts a year being exported, the bulk of it by alien merchants, although even then this branch of Boston's trade was overshadowed by the exports of hides from Newcastle, Hull and Southampton.[90] Nationally, the main demand for hides came from the domestic manufacture of leather and leather goods rather than from the overseas market.[91] Certainly, in comparison with Boston's wool trade, the port's exports of hides were of minor significance, representing, even at their peak, the hides of only around 3,300 animals, as opposed to the two million or more sheep whose wool was then being exported from the port. Hide exports were particularly high in the years 1319–21, perhaps because of the effects of the 'great bovine pestilence' which struck England from Easter 1319, and when, it has been claimed, England and Wales lost over 60% of their bovine populations to disease and slaughtering.[92] However, exports, which were now dominated by denizen merchants, soon returned to their former low levels; by the 1330s they barely reached a single last per year, and so this period is omitted from the graph below (Figure 2.2).

Figure 2.1 Hide exports from Boston, 1279–1548.

	Denizen			Alien			Total			
	Lasts	Dickers	Hides	Lasts	Dickers	hides	Lasts	Dickers	Hides	
19.5.1279–19.5.1280							15	11	0	
19.5.1280–13.4.1281							17	7	3	
13.4.1281–29.3.1282							13	14	0	

84 T.N.A., E122/10/5, f. 16v.

85 T.N.A., E356/24, mm. 9, 9d, 10, 10d; E356/25, mm. 7, 7d., 8, 8d.

86 T.N.A., E122/7/22, m. 8; Rigby, *Overseas Trade of Boston*, p. 138; T.N.A., E356/24, m. 8d.

87 T.N.A., E356/23, m. 9d.

88 T.N.A., E356/23, m. 10.

89 T.N.A., E122/10/1, m. 2

90 Jenks, *Enrolled Customs Accounts*, Part 1, pp. 1–13. For alien hide exports from 1303–1336, see Lloyd, *Alien Merchants in England*, Appendix I.

91 Britnell, *Britain and Ireland, 1050–1350*, pp. 419–20.

92 P. Slavin. 'The great bovine pestilence and its economic and environmental consequences in England and Wales, 1318–50', *Economic History Review*, 65 (2012), pp. 1239–66, at 1242.

	Denizen			Alien			Total			
	Lasts	Dickers	Hides	Lasts	Dickers	hides	Lasts	Dickers	Hides	
29.3.1282–18.4.1283							11	8	4	
18.4.1283–9.4.1284							21	8	8	
9.4.1284–25.3.1285							23	15	8	
25.3.1285–14.4.1286							8	8	1	
14.4.1286–6.4.1287							24	0	1	
6.4.1287–28.3.1288							15	7	7	
28.3.1288–10.4.1289							18	10	6	
10.4.1289–2.4.1290							19	15	8	
2.4.1290–Mich.1294	No returns									
Mich.1294–Mich.1295							22	14	8	
Mich.1295–Mich.1296							10	12	8	
Mich.1296–Mich.1297							13	8	1	
Mich.1297–7.5.1298							7	12	7	
7.5.1298–7.6.1299	No returns									
7.6.1299–Mich.1299							2	18	5	
Mich.1299–Mich.1300							2	15	2	
Mich.1300–Mich.1301							6	1	6	
Mich.1301–Mich.1302							14	8	6	
Mich.1302–30.9.1303				3	9	0	8	8	7	Note 1
30.9.1303–Mich.1304	0	3	8	22	8	5	22	12	3	
Mich.1304–Mich.1305	1	13	3	9	11	2	11	4	5	
Mich.1305–Mich.1306	2	5	2	18	4	5	20	9	7	
Mich.1306–Mich.1307	0	16	0	20	17	0	21	13	0	
Mich.1307–Mich.1308	1	16	0	11	3	4	12	19	4	
Mich.1308–Mich.1309	0	0	0	9	11	5	9	11	5	
Mich.1309–Mich.1310				2	16	1	2	16	1	Note 2
Mich.1310–Mich.1311				4	6	4	4	5	5	Note 3
Mich.1311–Mich.1312							12	10	1	
Mich.1312–Mich.1313							1	8	8	
Mich.1313–Mich.1314							0	0	0	
Mich.1314–Mich.1315							0	0	6	
Mich.1315–Mich.1316							2	9	0	
Mich.1316–Mich.1317							4	10	5	
Mich.1317–Mich.1318							0	0	0	
Mich.1318–Mich.1319							0	0	0	

	Denizen			Alien			Total			
	Lasts	Dickers	Hides	Lasts	Dickers	hides	Lasts	Dickers	Hides	
Mich.1319–Mich.1320							25	8	5	
Mich.1320–Mich–1321							23	14	0	
Mich.1321–Mich.1322							11	19	7	
Mich.1322–Mich.1323	0	8	5	1	0	0	1	8	5	
Mich.1323–Mich.1324	0	0	0	0	10	0	0	10	0	
Mich.1324–Mich.1325	1	0	0	3	9	2	4	9	2	
Mich.1325–Mich.1326	1	2	0	1	10	0	2	12	0	
Mich.1326–Mich.1327	0	10	0	0	10	8	1	0	8	
Mich.1327–27.8.1328	0	0	0	2	2	0	2	2	0	
27.8.1328–Mich.1329	1	18	4	1	19	5	3	17	9	
Mich.1329–Mich.1330	0	2	0	5	11	5	5	13	5	
Mich.1330–Mich.1331	0	0	0	0	7	5	0	7	5	
Mich.1331–Mich.1332	0	0	0	0	16	5	0	16	5	
Mich.1332–Mich.1333	0	0	0	0	3	0	0	3	0	
Mich.1333–Mich.1334	0	0	0	0	5	5	0	5	5	Note 4
Mich.1334–Mich.1335	0	2	5	0	1	0	0	3	5	
Mich.1335–15.7.1343	0	0	0	0	0	0	0	0	0	
15.7.1343–24.9.1350	No returns									
24.9.1350–30.9.1351							0	16	0	Note 5
30.9.1351–3.9.1352	0	0	0	0	0	0	0	0	0	
3.9.1352–Mich.1353	0	0	0	0	0	0	0	0	0	
Mich.1353–Mich.1354	0	5	4	0	5	4	0	5	4	
Mich.1354–Mich.1355	0	0	0	1	0	0	1	0	0	
Mich.1355–Mich.1356	0	0	0	0	0	2	0	0	2	
Mich.1356–Mich.1358	0	0	0	0	0	0	0	0	0	
Mich.1358–Mich.1359	0	0	0	0	0	3	0	0	3	
Mich.1359–Mich.1365	0	0	0	0	0	0	0	0	0	
Mich.1365–Mich.1366	0	0	0	0	12	2	0	12	2	
Mich.1366–Mich.1367	0	0	0	0	0	0	0	0	0	
Mich.1367–Mich.1368	0	0	0	0	0	5	0	0	5	
Mich.1368–Mich.1376	0	0	0	0	0	0	0	0	0	
Mich.1376–26.8.1377	0	0	0	0	4	0	0	4	0	
26.8.1377–Mich.1382	0	0	0	0	0	0	0	0	0	
Mich.1382–Mich.1383	0	7	0	0	7	0	0	7	0	
Mich.1383–Mich.1384	0	11	0	0	13	0	0	13	0	

	Denizen			Alien			Total		
	Lasts	Dickers	Hides	Lasts	Dickers	hides	Lasts	Dickers	Hides
Mich.1384–Mich.1390	0	0	0	0	0	0	0	0	0
Mich.1390–Mich.1391	0	0	0	0	4	2	0	4	2
Mich.1391–Mich.1433	0	0	0	0	0	0	0	0	0
Mich.1433–Mich.1434	0	0	0	0	1	2	0	1	2
Mich.1434–Mich.1435	0	1	0	0	0	0	0	1	0
Mich.1435–Mich.1439	0	0	0	0	0	0	0	0	0
Mich.1439–Mich.1440	0	2	0	0	0	0	0	2	0
Mich.1440–21.11.1448	0	0	0	0	0	0	0	0	0
21.11.1448–21.11.1449	0	0	0	0	1	0	0	1	0
2111.1449–Mich.1450	0	0	0	0	1	1	0	1	1
Mich.1450–Mich.1452	0	0	0	0	0	0	0	0	0
Mich.1452–Mich.1453	0	0	0	0	0	6	0	0	6
Mich.1453–Mich.1458	0	0	0	0	0	0	0	0	0
Mich.1458–15.12.1459	No returns								
15.12.1459–Mich.1464	0	0	0	0	0	0	0	0	0
Mich.1464–Mich.1465	0	2	0	0	2	0	0	2	0
Mich.1465–Mich.1498	0	0	0	0	0	0	0	0	0
Mich.1498–Mich.1499–	0	16	0	0	6	0	1	2	0
Mich.1499–Mich.1500	0	1	5	0	5	0	0	6	5
Mich.1500–Mich.1504	0	0	0	0	0	0	0	0	0
Mich.1504–Mich.1505	0	0	5	0	0	5	0	0	5
Mich.1505–Mich.1506	0	0	0	0	0	0	0	0	0
Mich.1506–Mich.1507	0	0	0	0	0	5	0	0	5
Mich.1507–Mich.1508	0	0	0	0	7	0	0	7	0
Mich.1508–Mich.1509	0	1	0	0	0	0	0	1	0
Mich.1509–Mich.1510	0	3	0	0	3	0	0	3	0
Mich.1510–Mich.1511	0	1	8	0	0	0	0	1	8
Mich.1511–Mich.1512	0	0	0	0	9	4	0	9	4
Mich.1512–Mich.1513	0	7	5	0	0	0	0	7	5
Mich.1513–Mich.1514	0	0	0	0	0	0	0	0	0
Mich.1514–Mich.1515	0	2	0	0	0	0	0	0	0
Mich.1515–Mich.1516	0	8	0	0	1	0	0	9	0
Mich.1516–Mich.1517	0	0	0	0	3	0	0	3	0
Mich.1517–Mich.1518	0	0	0	0	0	0	0	0	0
Mich.1518–Mich.1519	0	1	0	0	0	0	0	1	0

	Denizen			Alien			Total			
	Lasts	Dickers	Hides	Lasts	Dickers	hides	Lasts	Dickers	Hides	
Mich.1519–Mich.1520	0	0	0	0	0	0	0	0	0	
Mich.1520–Mich.1521	0	1	3	1	8	0	1	9	3	
Mich.1521–Mich.1525	0	0	0	0	0	0	0	0	0	
Mich.1525–Mich.1526	0	0	6	0	0	6	0	0	6	
Mich.1526–Mich.1527	0	0	0	0	0	0	0	0	0	
Mich.1527–Mich.1528	0	17	0	0	0	0	0	17	0	
Mich.1528–Mich.1529	0	0	0	0	8	0	0	8	0	
Mich.1529–Mich.1531	0	0	0	0	0	0	0	0	0	
Mich.1531–Mich.1532	0	0	0	1	6	5	1	6	5	
Mich.1532–Mich.1533	0	14	5	0	0	0	0	14	5	
Mich.1533–Mich.1535	0	0	0	0	0	0	0	0	0	
Mich.1535–Mich.1536	0	0	0	0	8	0	0	8	0	
Mich.1536–Mich.1537	0	7	0	1	4	0	1	11	0	
Mich.1537–Mich.1538	0	0	0	0	0	6	0	0	5	
Mich.1538–Mich.1548	0	0	0	0	0	0	0	0	0	

(Sources: 1279–1303: Jenks, Enrolled Customs Accounts, Part 1; 1303–1548: T.N.A., E356 Enrolled customs accounts)

Notes to Figure 2.1:

- Note 1. Figure for alien exports from 10 February 1303.
- Note 2. Figure for alien exports from 2 August 1310.
- Note 3. The total given for alien exports paying the new custom on hides in this year actually exceeds the joint total given for denizen and alien exports paying the ancient custom (T.N.A., E356/2, m. 29).
- Note 4. The total for 1333–4 includes 4 dickers of alien hides customed at the Lincoln staple (T.N.A., E356/8, m. 25; E356/10, m. 15).
- Note 5. Only a total of denizen and alien hides exported is available for 1350–1.

Figure 2.2 Hide exports from Boston, 1279–1330 (lasts).

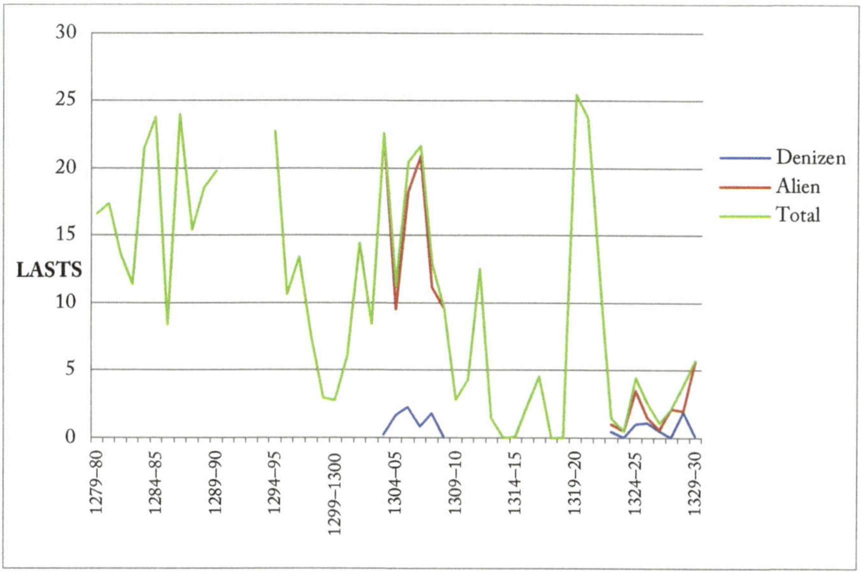

2.3 Alien cloth exports, 1303–43

While wool and hide exports were customed from 1275, levies on cloth exports were not imposed until the new custom of 1303, although this applied only to aliens; denizen exports remained free from custom until 1347 (see section 2.7, below). All non-denizen merchants, both those of the Hanseatic League and other aliens, paid the duty introduced in 1303. Their exports were charged at the rate of 2s. per standard cloth of assize (i.e. 24 yards long by 1½–2 yards wide) which had been dyed 'in grain', i.e. with an expensive dyestuff made from the dried bodies of kermes, an insect of Portugal and southern Spain. Cloths partly dyed in grain paid 1s. 6d. each, whilst those without grain paid 1s.[93] The new custom was not levied in 1309–10 or 1311–22, and no returns survive from 1343 to 1351 (as above).

Figures 3.1 and 3.2 give the totals of cloth liable to these duties which were exported from Boston between 1303 and 1343 by alien merchants. These included some Spaniards but were mainly men from Germany and the Low Countries.[94]

93 Gras, *Early English Customs System*, pp. 66, 263; Jenks, *Enrolled Customs Accounts*, Part 3, p.v.

94 W. Childs, 'The English export trade in cloth in the fourteenth century', in R. Britnell and J. Hatcher, eds, *Progress and problems in Medieval England: Essays in Honour of Edward Miller* (Cambridge, 1996), pp. 121–47, at 135–6; W. R. Childs, *Anglo-Castilian Trade in the Later Middle Ages* (Manchester, 1978), pp. 78, 84, 229.

In the early years of the century, Boston was the leading port in England for the export of cloths liable to these duties, with the volume of this trade there being even greater in volume than that of London. However, compared to the volume of imports (see section 2.4, below), exports charged with the specific duties on cloth which had been introduced in 1303 were of minor importance, amounting to around only a twentieth of the level of imports, even when they were at their maximum in the opening years of the fourteenth century. Unlike imports, which were dominated by cloths 'without grain', the majority of alien cloth exports in many years were charged at the highest rate of custom and were often referred to as 'scarlets', this being a reference to cloth's high quality rather than its colour. Much of these cloths must have been the product of the cloth industry at Lincoln, which was famous for its scarlets.[95] However, scarlets were by no means necessarily from Lincoln. Indeed, they could be both imported and exported, as in 1304–5, when 84¼ 'scarlets and other cloths in grain' were exported and 29 were imported. Merchants from a number of towns, including Leicester, Northampton, Norwich, York, Beverley, Newcastle, Banbury, Colchester, Bury St Edmunds and London, as well as Lincoln, sold cloth and clothing at Boston fair, some of which may have included scarlets.[96]

As we have seen, the new custom was suspended from 1311; by the time its collection was resumed, in 1322, alien exports of cloth at Boston charged with the specific duties on cloth had declined considerably from the earlier years of the century. It is tempting to link this falling off with the decline of Boston fair, of which it was said in 1334 that 'foreigners do not come as they used to'.[97] Certainly, St Botolph's fair, like other fairs in England, seems to have been in decline around this time.[98] However, it also likely that the decrease in Boston's alien cloth exports was linked to the difficulties being confronted by a number of English clothmaking towns in this period in the face of foreign and rural competition, with export markets being hit by warfare, trade embargoes, and piracy, with accompanying rising transaction costs, and a sharp decline in English wool production due to sheep disease.[99] Indeed,

95 J. W. F. Hill, *Medieval Lincoln*, (Stamford, 1990), p. 325; A. Kissane, *Civic Community in Medieval Lincoln: Urban Society and Economy in the Age of the Black Death, 1289–1409* (Woodbridge, 2017), p. 24; J. Munro, 'Scarlet', in G. R. Owen-Crocker, E. Coatsworth and M. Hayward, eds, *Encyclopedia of Dress and Textiles in the British Isles, c.450–1450* (Leiden, 2012), pp. 476–81; Childs, 'The English export trade in cloth', pp. 121–47 at 121–7.

96 T.N.A., E356/2, m. 28; Rigby, 'Medieval Boston', pp. 11–12. For scarlets made in Stamford, see Oldland, *The English Woollen Industry* pp. 85, 86.

97 *Calendar of Inquisitions Post Mortem*, volume 7, no. 625.

98 On the decline of Boston's fair and for references to other fairs, see Rigby, 'Medieval Boston', pp. 14–16 and E. W. Moore, *The Fairs of Medieval England: An Introductory Study* (Toronto, 1985), pp. 204–22, 289–90.

99 J. H. Munro, 'The "industrial crisis" of the English textile towns, *c.*1290-*c.*1330', in M. Prestwich, R. Britnell and R. Frame, eds, *Thirteenth Century England, VII: Proceedings of the Durham*

if anything, alien cloth exports held up better at Boston than elsewhere; it was 'one of the few ports from which they did not disappear altogether', although it is possible that exports by denizen merchants, which were not yet customed, may have partly compensated for the decline in the alien trade.[100]

A complication in interpreting the trends in alien cloth exports at Boston in this period is that much of the cloth sent from the port was not actually charged with the specific duties on cloth introduced in 1303, but was actually comprised of cheaper textiles which were charged with the general *ad valorem* duty of 3d. in the pound on miscellaneous goods that also formed part of the 1303 new custom (see section 2.6, below).[101] For instance, from 10 February to 29 September 1303, in addition to collecting the customs on alien exports of 101¾ scarlets, 22 cloths partly in grain and 162 cloths without grain (charged at 2s., 1s. 6d., and 1s. each, respectively), the Boston customs collectors also collected the 3d. in the pound custom from £ 4 of cloth of Beverley, £ 10 of Irish cloth, £ 147 of worsted and £ 1,152 of 'English cloth'. In addition, much other cloth was included in joint valuations for this custom with other exports such as salt. It is likely that, in total, the value of this cloth charged with the custom of 3d. in the pound exceeded that of the scarlets exported during this period.[102] Similarly, from Michaelmas 1308 to 28 August 1309, £ 1,699 of exports liable to the duty of 3d. in the pound were shipped from Boston, of which 30 % was made up of 'English cloth' and a further 32 % was comprised of joint valuations of cloth with honey, lead, eels, catskins and 'avoir dupois', (assorted goods sold by weight), which probably meant that this cloth equalled the total value of the exports of the scarlets and cloths without grain that were charged with the 1303 cloth custom during this period.[103] As we have seen, exports of cloth paying the 1303 cloth custom were in decline by the 1320s, but it seems unlikely that decline was compensated for by any increase in cloths charged with the custom of 3d. in the pound, since the value of exports charged with the *ad valorem* duty itself declined by two thirds between 1303–08 and 1322–27 (see Figure 6.1, below).

Conference, 1997 (Woodbridge, 1999), pp. 103–42, at 119–21, 135–8; Slavin, 'Mites and merchants', pp. 905–8; Oldland, *English Woollen Industry*, pp. 75, 98, 113–14.

100 Lloyd, *Alien Merchants in England*, pp. 46–7; Childs, 'The English export trade in cloth', pp. 133–4.

101 Munro, 'The "industrial crisis" of the English textile towns', p. 118; Childs, 'The English export trade in cloth', pp. 128–9.

102 T.N.A., E122/5/7. A scarlet cloth of assize could cost as much as £ 9 12s. in this period (Carus-Wilson, *Medieval Merchant Venturers*, p. 242).

103 T.N.A., E122/6/2; E356/2, m. 29d.

Figure 3.1 Alien cloth exports from Boston, 1303–43, liable to the specific duties on cloth.

	Scarlets and cloth in grain	Grain intermixed	Without grain	Total
10.2.1303–Mich.1303	101.75	22	162	285.75
Mich.1303–Mich.1304	57	0	14.5	71.5
Mich.1304–Mich.1305	84.25	0	155	239.25
Mich.1305–Mich.1306	92	1	76	169
Mich.1306–Mich.1307	70.5	1	67	138.5
Mich.1307–Mich.1308	92.5	0	76.5	169
Mich.1308–28.8.1309	48	0	11.5	59.5
28.8.1309–2.8.1310	No returns			
2.8.1310–Mich.1310	21.5	0	19	40.5
Mich.1310–27.10.1311	52	1	11	64
27.10.1311–20.7.1322	No returns			
20.7.1322–Mich.1323	26.5	0	12.5	39
Mich.1323–Mich.1324	29	0	0	29
Mich.1324–Mich.1325	47.5	0.5	2.5	50.5
Mich.1325–Mich.1326	6.5	0	4	10.5
Mich.1326–Mich.1327	29.5	0	3.5	33
Mich.1327–27.8.1328	9.5	0	5	14.5
27.8.1328–Mich.1329	16	0	50	66
Mich.1329–Mich.1330	27.5	0	19.5	47
Mich.1330–Mich.1331	9.5	0	9.5	19
Mich.1331–Mich.1332	9	0	7.5	16.5
Mich.1332–Mich.1333	9.5	0	7	16.5
Mich.1333–Mich.1334	14	0	9	23
Mich.1334–Mich.1335	5.5	0	1	6.5
Mich.1335–23.8.1336	21.5	0	0	21.5
23.8.1336–Mich.1337	5.5	0	2	7.5
Mich.1337–Mich.1338	5	0	0	5
Mich.1338–Mich.1339	1	0	0	1
Mich.1339–16.7.1340	0	0	0	0
16.7.1340–Mich.1341	0.5	0	0	0.5
Mich.1341–16.6.1342	0	0	0	0
16.6.1342–15.7.1343	0	0	0	0

(Source: T.N.A., E356 Enrolled customs accounts)

Figure 3.2 Alien cloth exports from Boston, 1303–43, liable to the specific duties on cloth.

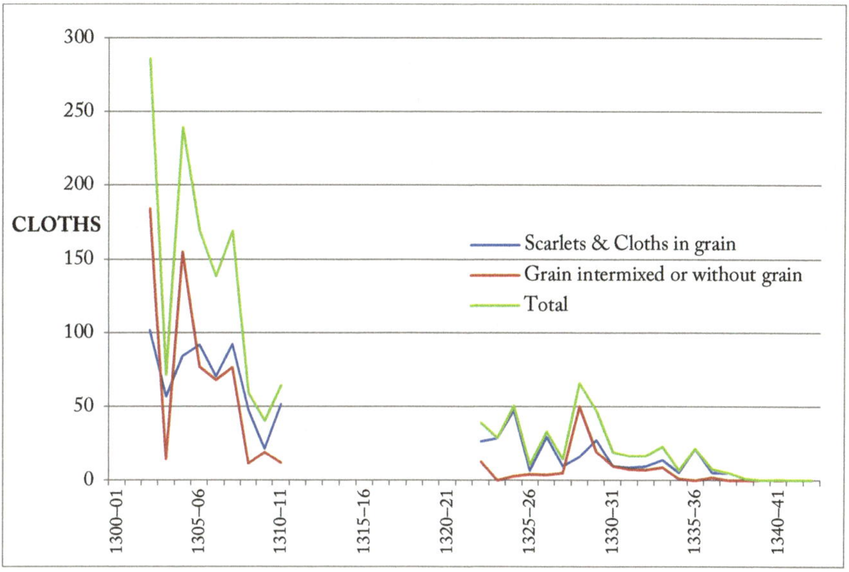

2.4 Alien cloth imports, 1303–1367

The 1303 new custom also included a levy on cloth imports by alien merchants, which, as we have already noted, were much greater in volume than their cloth exports. The custom on imports was charged at the same rate as that on exports, i.e. at 2s. per cloth of assize dyed in grain, 1s. 6d. per cloth partly dyed in grain, and 1s. per cloth without grain.[104] This duty was paid by all non-denizen merchants, both those of the Hanseatic League and other aliens. The custom was not levied from 1309 to 1310, or 1311 to 1322, and no returns survive from 1343 to 1351 (as above). Fortunately, unlike much of the cloth exported from Boston, woollen cloth was not included in the imports by alien merchants charged with the *ad valorem* duty of 3d. in the pound, which makes it much easier to follow the fluctuations in this branch of the alien trade.

Figures 4.1 and 4.2 give the totals of cloth imported to Boston by alien merchants, to the nearest cloth, between 1303 and 1367. In the earliest years of the new custom, about 12,000 cloths a year were imported into England by aliens, most of it manufactured in Flanders and Brabant.[105] Of these, about a quarter passed

104 Gras, *Early English Customs System*, pp. 66, 263; Jenks, *Enrolled Customs Accounts*, Part 3, p.v.

105 Lloyd, *Alien Merchants in England*, p. 111; Oldland, *English Woollen Industry*, p. 75.

through Boston, which meant that the port was second only to London in the trade.[106] Alien cloth imports to Boston, which were dominated by cloths without grain, were at their peak in the years after 1328, when military and social conflict abated in Flanders, with over 4,200 cloths a year being imported. However, the long-term trend, at Boston, as nationally, was one of decline, a trend accelerated by the prohibition on cloth imports to England in 1337, when Edward III sought to bring pressure on Flanders at the opening of the Hundred Years' War. Even though, in practice, the Crown could licence exemptions from this prohibition, the trade shrank dramatically and from 1365 the enrolled accounts of the new custom cease to include any mention of alien cloth imports.[107] However, the 1366–67 account for the custom on cloth exports which had been introduced in 1347 (see section 2.7) does include alien cloth imports, whilst the accounts for this custom for 1365–66, 1367–71 and 1390 include totals for cloths which are said to have been 'imported or exported' (see the notes to Figure 7.1).

Figure 4.1 Alien cloth imports to Boston, 1303–67.

	Scarlets and cloths in grain	Grain intermixed	Without grain	Total	
10.2.1303–Mich.1303	7	45	1282.75	1334.75	
Mich.1303–Mich.1304	19	179	2391.5	2589.5	
Mich.1304–Mich.1305	29	97	4041	4167	
Mich.1305–Mich.1306	4	74	2379.5	2457.5	
Mich.1306–Mich.1307	13	46	3240	3299	
Mich.1307–Mich.1308	23	79	2876.5	2978.5	
Mich.1308–28.8.1309	9.5	35	3511.5	3556	
28.8.1309–2.8.1310	No returns				
2.8.1310–Mich.1310	7	0	2048	2055	
Mich.1310–27.10.11	6	10	3297	3313	
27.10.1311–20.7.1322	No returns				
20.7.1322–Mich.1323	1	3.5	1352.5	1357	
Mich.1323–Mich.1324	7	50	3326.5	3383.5	
Mich.1324–Mich.1325	23	51	3210.5	3284.5	Note 1
Mich.1325–Mich.1326	1	11	1199	1211	
Mich.1326–Mich.1327	7	27	2311	2345	
Mich.1327–27.8.1328	9	47	4886.5	4942.5	
27.8.1328–Mich.1329	21	38	4554.5	4603.5	

106 T.N.A., E356/2.

107 Rigby, 'Medieval Boston', p. 15; Lloyd, *Alien Merchants in England*, p. 53; Oldland, *English Woollen Industry*, p 115–16.

	Scarlets and cloths in grain	Grain intermixed	Without grain	Total	
Mich.1329–Mich.1330	1	10	1939.5	1950.5	
Mich.1330–Mich.1331	36	47	6231	6314	
Mich.1331–Mich.1332	6	11	3602	3619	
Mich.1332–Mich.1333	7	4	1076	1087	
Mich.1333–Mich.1334	12	2	1056	1070	
Mich.1334–Mich.1335	0	1	170.5	171.5	
Mich.1335–23.8.1336	0	0	3961.5	3961.5	
23.8.1336–Mich.1337	0	0	0	0	
Mich.1337–Mich.1338	4	1	123	128	
Mich.1338–Mich.1339	0	0	0	0	
Mich.1389–16.7.1340	0	0	32	32	
16.7.1340–Mich.1341	0	0	168	168	
Mich.1341–16.6.1342	0	0	0	0	
16.6.1342–15.7.1343	1	2	57	60	
15.7.1342–Mich.1351	No returns				
Mich.1351–Mich.1352	3	0	151.5	154.5	
Mich.1352–Mich.1353	0	0	105.5	105.5	
Mich.1353–Mich.1354	0	1	1089.25	1090.25	Note 2
Mich.1354–Mich.1355	1	0	144	145	
Mich.1355–Mich.1356	1	1.5	308	310.5	
Mich.1356–30.9.1357	0	2	858.5	860.5	
30.9.1357–Mich.1358	0	0	96.75	96.75	
Mich.1358–Mich.1359	3	0	1088	1091	
Mich.1359–Mich.1360	0	0	339	339	
Mich.1360–Mich.1361	0	0	85.75	85.75	
Mich.1361–Mich.1362	0	0	618	618	
Mich.1362–Mich.1363	0	0	484.25	484.25	
Mich.1363–2.10.1364	0	0	6	6	Note 3
2.10.1364–20.10.1365	3	7	790	800	
20.10.1365–Mich.1366	0	0	0	0	
Mich.1366–Mich.1367	0	0	0	118	Note 4

(Source: T.N.A., E356 Enrolled customs accounts)

Notes to Figure 4.1:

- Note 1. The enrolled account for Michaelmas 1324 to 1 February 1325 includes the 113s. custom paid on 113 alien cloths without grain imported (T.N.A., E356/2, m. 46); this is given as 103 cloths in Jenks, *Enrolled Customs Accounts*, Part 1, p. 242.

- Note 2. The account for 29 January to Michaelmas 1354 includes 770¼ cloths without grain which paid 1s. custom each and which are said to have been imported and exported. They are included here in the column for imports for the year from Michaelmas 1353 (T.N.A., E356/9, m. 24).
- Note 3. The new custom account for 1363–4 notes 1,789 cloths imported and exported by Hanseatic merchants (T.N.A., E356/9, m. 24d.), but since the account for the 1347 cloth custom gives 1,783 cloths as exported by the Hansards in this year (T.N.A., E356/7, m. 11), this means that 6 of the 1,789 cloths were imported by Hansards.
- Note 4. The new custom account for 1366–7 (T.N.A., E356/9, m. 24d.) does not mention any alien cloth imports, but the enrolled account for the 1347 custom on cloth exports (T.N.A., E356/7, m. 12d.) includes 118 cloths without grain as being imported by aliens and so these are included here.

Figure 4.2 Alien cloth imports to Boston, 1303–67.

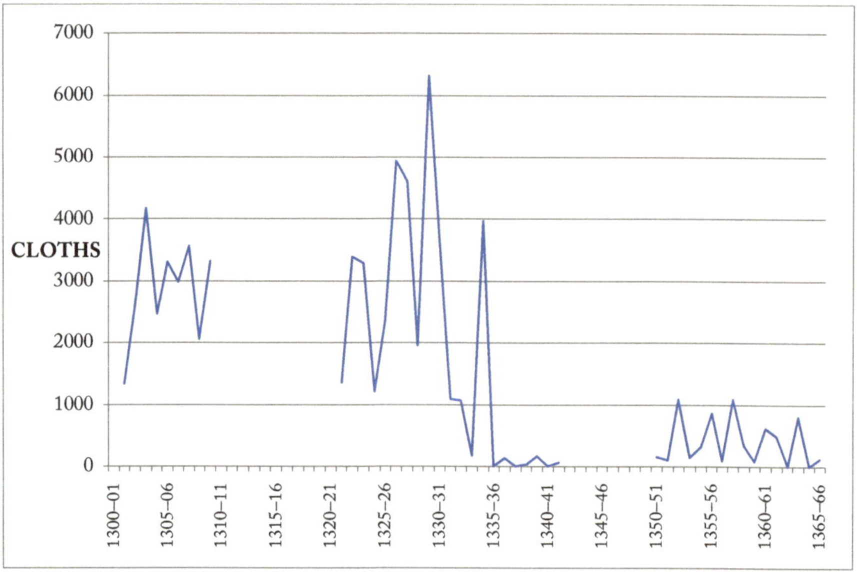

2.5 Alien wax imports, 1303–1548

In general, historians have paid little attention to the market for wax within the medieval economy, yet there was a large and growing demand for wax in late medieval England, mainly for lighting, but also for other uses, such as sealing documents. Whilst poorer households used tallow and rushes for lighting, richer ones preferred beeswax candles. In particular, wax was bought for use in churches. Imports of wax into England, which came mainly from the forests of eastern Europe via the Baltic ports, were substantial. In 1309, when imports slumped and the price of wax had doubled, Hanseatic merchants were accused of having deliberately created a shortage of it, although they subsequently proved their innocence.[108] Sapoznik has argued that imports constituted only a small part of the total wax consumed in England, but nevertheless they constituted a high-quality product which was particularly in demand from wealthier ecclesiastical institutions, such as Bolton Priory (Yorkshire) and Durham Priory, both of which purchased wax at Boston fair in the early fourteenth century.[109] Wax imports were customed from 1303, when the new custom included a specific levy on alien imports of wax. This allows us to follow the fluctuations in this trade. The custom was charged at the rate of 1s. per quintal, which first contained 112 lbs., but at some later point in the fourteenth century was reduced to 100 lbs.[110] All non-denizen merchants paid this duty, with the Hansards dominating the trade, importing wax directly from the east or re-shipping it via the Low Countries.[111] The custom was not levied from 1309 to 1310, or 1311 to 1322, and no returns survive from 1343 to 1351 (as above), or from December 1372 to August 1377, when the custom was farmed.[112]

Figures 5.1 and 5.2 give the numbers of quintals of wax imported by alien merchants at Boston from 1303. In the early years of the new custom, when around 300 quintals a year were imported by aliens through Boston, the port was second only to London in the trade. Alien wax imports reached their peak in the early 1320s, at around 400 quintals a year, and remained buoyant in the 1330s, when Boston actually

108 P. Dollinger, *The German Hansa* (London, 1970), pp. 56–7; C. Jahnke, 'The Baltic trade', in D. J. Harreld, ed., *A Companion to the Hanseatic League* (Leiden, 2015), pp. 194–220, at 218–20.

109 A. Sapoznik, 'Bees in the medieval economy: religious observance and the production, trade and consumption of wax in England, c.1300–1555', *Economic History Review*, 72 (2019), pp. 1152–74; *The Bolton Priory Compotus, 1286–1325, Together with a Priory Account Roll for 1377–1378*, eds I. Kershaw, D. M. Smith and T. N. Cooper (Yorkshire Archaeological Society Record Series, 154 (2000)), pp. 213, 362, 383, 405; *Extracts from the Account Rolls of the Abbey of Durham*, volume I, ed. J. T. Fowler (Surtees Society, 99 (1898)), pp. 495–6, 512.

110 Gras, *Early English Customs System*, pp. 66, 263; Jenks, *Enrolled Customs Accounts*, Part 1, p. vi; Jenks, *Enrolled Customs Accounts*, Part 3, p.v. The earliest enrolled accounts of the 1303 new custom specify that a quintal contained 112 lbs (T.N.A., E356/2, mm. 28, 28d.); the Boston account for 1491–2 states that the 7,400 lbs of wax imported by Hansards were the equivalent of 74 quintals, i.e. 100 lbs per quintal (T.N.A., E356/23, m. 8).

111 Sapoznik, 'Bees in the medieval economy', p. 1164; T. H. Lloyd, *England and the German Hanse, 1157–1611: A Study of their Trade and Commercial Diplomacy* (Cambridge, 1991), p. 40.

112 *Calendar of Fine Rolls, 1369–77*, pp. 198, 404; Carus-Wilson and Coleman, *England's Export Trade*, p. 79.

replaced the capital as the main port in England for this trade.[113] However, from 1338, wax imports at Boston declined dramatically, rarely reaching 90 quintals a year, even between 1353 and 1373, when the Lynn and Boston customs jurisdictions were merged. By the early fifteenth century, the trade had virtually disappeared (the years after 1408 are therefore not given in graph form in Figure 5.2), even though other branches of the Hanse's trade were flourishing in the port. London took an increasing share of the wax trade, particularly from the last quarter of the fifteenth century, when, even allowing for the reduction in the size of the quintals used for customs, the trade nationally reached new heights, with London importing between 1,000 and 3,500 quintals a year. In contrast, at Boston there were many years when there were no wax imports at all.[114]

There was no specific custom on the wax imports of denizen merchants and so their wax imports are only visible in the surviving particular accounts in valuations for the subsidy of poundage (see section 2.9, below).[115] As denizen merchants penetrated into the Baltic in the late fourteenth century, their imports through Boston included significant amounts of wax. For instance, an account of tunnage and poundage shows that in the nine months from 1 March 1390, denizens were responsible for around 90 % of the wax imported at Boston.[116] However, such imports did not compensate for the decline in the alien trade, and even denizen wax imports declined in the fifteenth century.

Figure 5.1 Alien wax imports to Boston, 1303–1548 (quintals).

10.2.1303–Mich. 1303	312.75
Mich. 1303–Mich. 1304	212.75
Mich.1304–Mich.1305	317.625
Mich.1305–Mich.1306	489.125
Mich.1306–Mich.1307	368
Mich.1307–Mich.1308	216.5
Mich.1308–28.8.1309	148.75
28.8.1309–2.8.1310	No returns
2.8.1310–Mich.1310	126.5
Mich.1310–27.10.1311	248
27.10–1311–20.7.1322	No returns
20.7.1322–Mich.1322	151.25
20.7.1322–Mich.1323	691.5
Mich.1323–Mich.1324	582.5
Mich.1324–Mich.1325	331.25
Mich.1325–Mich.1326	361.5
Mich.1326–Mich.1327	263.75
Mich.1327–Mich.1328	183.75
Mich.1328–Mich.1329	488
Mich.1329–Mich.1330	98
Mich.1330–Mich.1331	460.5
Mich.1331–Mich.1332	200
Mich.1332–Mich.1333	289.5
Mich.1333–Mich.1334	333

113 Lloyd, *Alien Merchants in England*, p. 39 and Appendix I.

114 Lloyd, *England and the German Hanse*, p. 80. 382; Sapoznik, 'Bees in the medieval economy', p. 1164.

115 See for instance, T.N.A., E122/7/17; E122/7/21; E122/7/24; E122/7/27; E122/10/26; Rigby, *Overseas Trade of Boston*, pp. 39, 42, 43, 92–9, 167, 180.

116 T.N.A., E122/7/21; Rigby, *Overseas Trade of Boston*, pp. 84–113.

Mich.1334–Mich.1335	157.75
Mich.1335–23.8.1336	198.75
28.8.1336–Mich.1337	16.25
Mich.1337–Mich.1338	126.25
Mich.1338–Mich.1339	40
Mich.1339–16.7.1340	32.5
16.7.1340–Mich.1341	8.75
Mich.1341–16.6.1342	0
16.6.1342–15.7.1343	24.75
15.7.1343–Mich.1351	No returns
Mich.1351–Mich.1352	0
Mich.1352–Mich.1353	8.75
Mich.1353–Mich.1354	188
Mich.1354–Mich.1355	17
Mich.1355–Mich.1356	0
Mich.1356–30.9.1357	61.5
30.9.1357–Mich.1358	10.5
Mich.1358–Mich.1359	77.8
Mich.1359–Mich.1360	0
Mich.1360–Mich.1361	34.75
Mich.1361–Mich.1362	16
Mich.1362–Mich.1363	35.5
Mich.1363–2.10.1364	16.25
2.10.1364–20.10.1365	59.54
20.10.1365–Mich.1366	61
Mich.1366–Mich.1367	61.75
Mich.1367–Mich.1368	48
Mich.1368–Mich.1369	37.5
Mich.1369–Mich.1370	35.625
Mich.1370–Mich.1371	15
Mich.1371–Mich.1372	87.375
Mich.1372–24.12.1372	82.375
24.12.1372–26.8.1377	No returns
26.8.1377–Mich.1378	16
Mich.1378–Mich.1379	21
Mich.1379–Mich.1380	20.5
Mich.1380–Mich.1381	18
Mich.1381–Mich.1382	40
Mich.1382–Mich.1383	6
Mich.1383–Mich.1384	0

Mich.1384–Mich.1385	3
Mich.1385–Mich.1386	25
Mich.1386–26.11.1387	7.25
26.11.1387–Mich.1388	12
Mich.1388–Mich.1389	48.25
Mich.1389–Mich.1390	9.125
Mich.1390–Mich.1391	8
Mich.1391–Mich.1392	68.875
Mich.1392–Mich.1393	49.75
Mich.1393–Mich.1394	1
Mich.1394–Mich.1395	39.875
Mich.1395–Mich.1396	0
Mich.1396–Mich.1397	0
Mich.1397–Mich.1398	2.5
Mich.1398–Mich.1399	16.38
Mich.1399–Mich.1400	5.5
Mich.1400–Mich.1401	5.5
Mich.1401–Mich.1402	7.625
Mich.1402–Mich.1403	11
Mich.1403–Mich.1404	0
Mich.1404–Mich.1405	0
Mich.1405–3.11.1406	0
3.11.1406–Mich.1407	0
Mich.1407–Mich.1408	11.75
Mich.1408–Mich.1409	6
Mich.1409–Mich.1410	0
Mich.1410–Mich.1411	0
Mich.1411–Mich.1412	0
Mich.1412–Mich.1413	0
Mich.1413–Mich.1414	0.25
Mich.1414–Mich.1415	0
Mich.1415–Mich.1416	2.5
Mich.1416–Mich.1417	0
Mich.1417–Mich.1418	0
Mich.1418–Mich.1419	3.125
Mich.1419–10.10.1420	1.5
10.10.1420–Mich.1421	0
Mich.1421–31.8.1422	0
1.9.1422–Mich.1423	3.5
Mich.1423–Mich.1424	0.75

Mich.1424–Mich.1425	0	10.10.1436–11.11.1437	7.28
Mich.1425–Mich.1426	0	11.11.1437–Mich.1438	14.5
Mich.1426–Mich.1427	0	Mich.1438–Mich.1439	2.5
Mich.1427–Mich.1428	0	Mich.1439–Mich.1491	0
Mich.1428–1.11.1429	2.125	Mich.1491–Mich.1492	74
1.11.1429–1.11.1430	10.75	Mich.1492–Mich.1503	0
1.11.1430–20.10.1431	0	Mich.1503–Mich.1504	8.5
20.10.1431–Mich.1432	0	Mich.1504–Mich.1517	0
Mich.1432–Mich.1433	28.5	Mich.1517–Mich.1518	4.5
Mich.1433–Mich.1434	0	Mich.1518–Mich.1532	0
Mich.1434–Mich.1435	0	Mich.1532–Mich.1533	16
Mich.1435–10.10.1436	0	Mich.1533–Mich.1548	0

(Source: T.N.A., E356 Enrolled customs accounts)

Figure 5.2 Alien wax imports to Boston, 1303–1408.

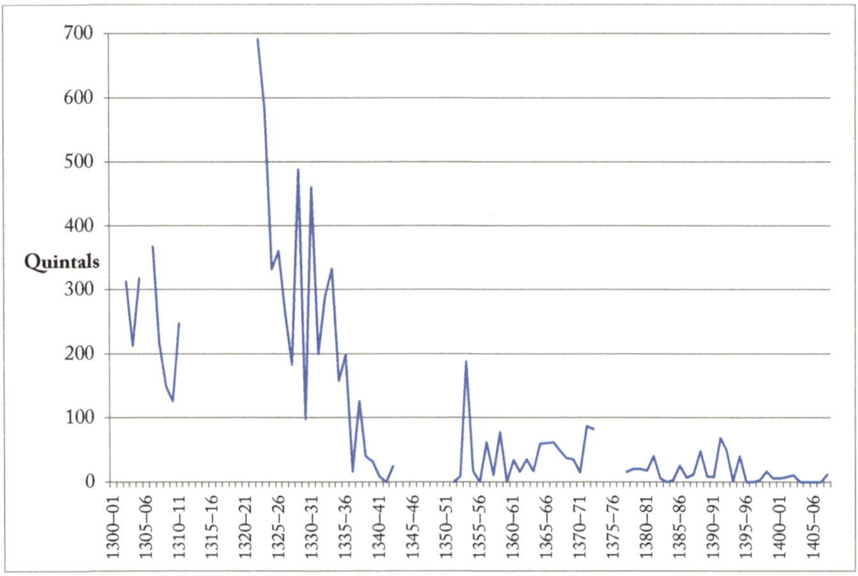

2.6 Miscellaneous alien imports and exports, 1303–1548

Besides the duties introduced in 1303 for alien merchants on their exports of wool, woolfells, hides and cloth, and on their imports of cloth and wax, the new custom also included an *ad valorem* duty of 3d. in the pound on other goods imported or exported by aliens.[117] Figures 6.1 and 6.2 give the totals of alien imports and exports liable to the custom of 3d. in the pound, to the nearest pound, which were made by alien merchants at Boston between 1303 and 1548. We do not have returns for the custom from 1309 to 1310, or 1311 to 1322, when it was not levied, or from 1343 to 1351, when it was granted to a consortium of English merchants (see above). Nor are there any returns for this custom for Boston between December 1372 and August 1377, when it was part of a customs farm.[118] Before 1335, the enrolled accounts for Boston provide us with separate totals for the imports and exports liable to this duty, which allows us to see the balance of trade in this branch of the port's commerce (see Figure 6.3).[119] However, after this date the enrolled accounts only include the combined total of imports and exports which incurred this *ad valorem* charge, and so the balance of trade in miscellaneous imports and exports can only be calculated in those years for which particular customs accounts survive.[120]

All non-denizen merchants normally paid this duty, both those of the Hanseatic League as well as other aliens. However, following the 1474 Treaty of Utrecht, which resolved the Anglo-Hanseatic conflict that had broken out in 1468, the Hansards were granted £ 10,000 compensation for their commercial losses, which was to be paid in the form of a customs exemption.[121] As a result, in the decade from Michaelmas 1475, the enrolled customs accounts distinguished the trade of Hanseatic merchants which was liable to the custom of 3d. in the pound from that of other aliens. The Hansards' miscellaneous trade in Boston is also distinguished from that of other aliens in three accounts of the 1490s and two from the late 1530s.[122] The value of this Hanseatic trade is given in the notes to Figure 6.1. Another group of merchants whose trade is distinguished in the enrolled accounts are the merchants of Veere (or 'Caumfer') in Zeeland, who, as a result of the support offered by the lord of Veere to Edward IV when he recovered the English throne in 1471, were granted various privileges until the end of the reign.[123] A number of the enrolled accounts within the period from 22 December 1471 to 9 April 1483

117 Gras, *Early English Customs System*, pp. 66, 263; Jenks, *Enrolled Customs Accounts*, Part 3, p.v.

118 See footnote 112, above.

119 There are also separate particular accounts for imports and for exports liable to this duty during this period (T.N.A., E122/5/7; E122/5/9; E122/5/10; E122/6/2; E122/6/3; E122/6/21; E122/6/22), although those for 1310 (E122/6/6) and 1334 (E122/7/4) include both imports and exports.

120 Although the enrolled accounts of all English ports originally gave separate totals for imports and exports liable to the custom of 3d. in the pound, there was no national policy about when these were replaced by a single combined total, with some ports adopting the new accounting practice as early as the mid-1320s (see Lloyd, *Alien Merchants in England*, Appendix I).

121 Lloyd, *England and the German Hanse*, p. 216; Jenks, *Enrolled Customs Accounts*, Part 9, p. xii.

122 T.N.A., E356/22, mm. 2–4d; E356/23, mm. 8, 8d., 9d.

123 C. Ross, *Edward IV* (New Haven, 1997), p. 160; Jenks, *Enrolled Customs Accounts*, part 9, p.v.

specify the total value of imports and exports by merchants of Veere which were liable to the custom of 3d. in the pound; the value of these goods is given in the notes to Figure 6.1.

The liability of alien merchants to the custom of 3d. in the pound changed from 6 April 1539, when aliens (including the Hansards) benefitted from a royal order of 13 February which introduced a seven-year experiment whereby, with the exception of their wool exports, aliens were only required to pay customs and subsidies on their goods at the same rates as the king's own subjects.[124] From September 1540, this equalization of denizen and alien rates was qualified by the ruling that it only applied to alien goods which were imported or exported on English ships, although this proviso did not apply to Hanseatic merchants. This change provoked retaliation from the Emperor, which hit England's trade with the Low Countries, including that with Holland and Flanders, but the conflict was resolved from June 1542, when the merchants of Spain and the imperial Low Countries were also exempted from the 1540 ruling about using English ships.[125] However, whilst denizen and aliens paid the same rates of custom and subsidy during this seven-year period, meaning that aliens were exempt from the 1303 custom of 3d. in the pound on miscellaneous goods, Boston's enrolled customs accounts from 6 April 1539 to Michaelmas 1546 continued to note how much aliens would have paid if they had been charged with this custom. This allows us to calculate the total value of their miscellaneous trade. Surprisingly, given that this exemption should have applied to all aliens, the enrolled accounts for Boston record that the Hansards were charged with this custom in the port for the entire year of 1538–9, when their goods made up £ 424 of £ 1,338 11s. 4d. of alien imports and exports, and again in 1539–40, when their goods comprised £ 324 6s. 8d. of £ 726 7s. 8d. of alien imports and exports. The Hanseatic component of this trade was not distinguished from that of other aliens after Michaelmas 1540, although, in practice, all miscellaneous alien imports and exports through Boston from Michaelmas 1541 to Michaelmas 1545 were by non-Hansards.[126] As the order introducing the equalization of rates had noted, reducing the customs and subsidies paid by aliens to that paid by denizen merchants would be to the king's own 'detriment and loss'. Royal officials correctly calculated that the reduction of alien

124 For the text of this order, see *Tudor Royal Proclamations, Volume I: The Early Tudors, 1485–1553*, eds P. L. Hughes and J. F. Larkin (New Haven, 1964), pp. 281–3 and Schanz, *Englische Handelspolitik*, II, pp. 602–4.

125 *Letters and Papers Foreign and Domestic, Henry VIII, Volume 16: 1540–41*, nos 374, 524, 864; *Letters and Papers Foreign and Domestic, Henry VIII, Volume 17: 1542*, no. 440. The equalization of customs rates is discussed in Lloyd, *England and the German Hanse*, pp. 269–71, although it is dated there as being introduced from 6 April 1538 (p. 269).

126 From Michaelmas 1541 to Michaelmas 1545, the value of alien imports and exports not charged with poundage was the same as that for alien imports and exports not charged with the custom of 3d. in the pound. Since the Hansards were not liable to poundage, it follows that all of these goods were shipped by non-Hanseatic aliens (T.N.A., E356/27, mm. 4–6).

duties in this period (including those paid on cloth as well as the *ad valorem* duty) had cost the Crown around £ 17 of revenues in Boston from 6 April 1539 to the following Michaelmas.[127]

Figures 6.1 and 6.2 show the fluctuations in Boston's alien miscellaneous trade between 1303 and 1548. In the early years of the fourteenth century, Boston was second only to London amongst England's ports in the scale of its alien miscellaneous trade, which was valued at around £ 12,500 a year in the five years from Michaelmas 1303, i.e. about half the level of this branch of trade in the capital.[128] As Figure 6.3 shows, this branch of Boston's trade was, as in England's other ports, comprised mainly of imports, which made up over two thirds of miscellaneous imports and exports in this period. To identify the goods which paid this custom, we must turn to Boston's particular accounts. That for February to Michaelmas 1303, for instance, shows that the main imports to the port were stockfish (i.e. dried cod) and fish oil, which were brought from Bergen (Norway) by the Hansards, particularly those of Lübeck. These overshadowed the value of other eastern European and Scandinavian goods, such as furs, skins, copper, cinders and boards.[129] Boston at this time was benefitting from a Hanseatic boycott of Lynn, which had previously been the main port in the Anglo-Norwegian trade, following a conflict over their privileges there.[130] The role of Scandinavian merchants, including the Danes, in this trade was relatively minor at this time, and declined even further in the course of the fourteenth century.[131] Other significant imports in this period included iron and steel, metal goods such as swords, helmets, brass pans and batteryware (i.e. hammered metal goods, often from Dinant), as well as a huge range of cloths (including linen and canvas), foodstuffs (garlic and honey), raw materials (boards and cinders) and manufactured goods such as millstones and quern-stones. As we have seen, the most important single commodity amongst Boston's miscellaneous exports was cloth (see section 2.3, above), which, from February to Michaelmas 1303 and Michaelmas 1308 to 28 August 1309, made up around a third of the value of miscellaneous exports, quite apart from joint valuations with other goods such as honey, lead and eels. Second in value was

127 *Letters and Papers Foreign and Domestic, Henry VIII, Volume 16: 1540–41*, no. 90.

128 Lloyd, *Alien Merchants in England*, Appendix I.

129 T.N.A., E122/5/9; E122/6/5; Burkhardt, 'The German Hanse and Bergen', pp. 64–5. On the Bergen trade, see also M. Burkhardt., *Der hansische Bergenhandel in Spätmittelalter: Handel-Kaufleute-Netwerke* (Köln, 2009). For furs, see E. M. Veale, *The English Fur Trade in the Later Middle Ages* (Oxford, 1966), p. 68.

130 A. Nedkvitne, *The German Hansa and Bergen, 1100–1600* (Bergen, 2014), pp. 75–6; Lloyd, *England and the German Hanse*, p. 40.

131 W. R. Childs, 'Medieval English trade in the North Sea: Denmark and Jutland, *c* 1300–1500', in E. Damgaard, M. Guldberg and P. Holm, eds, *A North Sea Region: West Jutland and the World, II (Proceedings of the Lemvig Conference, April 3–5, 1995)* (Esbjerg, 1998), pp. 47–74, at 58–65.

salt, which in 1308–9 accounted for 23 % of exports (excluding joint valuations), with Boston, which was conveniently placed for England's leading salt-producing region of Norfolk and Lincolnshire, being pre-eminent in this branch of the country's alien trade. Other exports included foodstuffs (including wheat, malt, cheese, butter, beans and honey) and Derbyshire lead, although lead accounted for less than 5 % of exports in 1308–9.[132]

Boston's alien miscellaneous trade, particularly that in imports, remained buoyant for much of the 1320s and 1330s with the port seemingly benefitting from the decline of this branch of trade in London at this time.[133] Its value averaged around £ 7,400 a year in the 1320s and still reached almost £ 6,600 a year from 1330 to 1336, with a particular account for the first six months of 1334 suggesting that the type of goods being imported and exported, if not their volume, remained as before.[134] As we have seen, the new custom was farmed from 1343 to 1351 and then, from 1353 to 1373, the Boston customs administration was merged with that of Lynn. During the 1350s and 1360s, the alien miscellaneous trade of the two combined ports was still buoyant, averaging over £ 9,000 a year and, between 1361 and 1366, even reaching over £ 11,000 a year. These totals are obviously inflated by the inclusion of Lynn's trade. Nevertheless, in the two years from Michaelmas 1351, i.e. before the Lynn and Boston jurisdictions were merged, the goods charged with the custom of 3d. in the pound at Lynn made up only a quarter of the combined total value of this trade in the two ports, and so it seems likely that the bulk of miscellaneous alien imports and exports went through Boston itself.[135] Certainly, in the five years from 1377, when we have separate figures for Boston once more, the level of the port's trade almost rivalled the peak years of the early fourteenth century, with almost £ 11,000 a year of miscellaneous alien goods being imported and exported.

After this date, this branch of Boston's trade went into a long-term decline, although it was still valued at around £ 6–8,000 in the last two decades of the fourteenth century. By this time, the composition of this trade was very different from that of the early fourteenth century. Whereas exports had once made up over a quarter of the alien miscellaneous trade, by the late fourteenth and early fifteenth century, they had shrunk to around only 5 % of the trade. They were mainly made up of 'narrow cloth', which was exempt from the 1347 custom charged on standard cloths of assize (see section 2.7, below), blankets and caps, along with a variety of other goods of little total value, including lead, alabaster images (probably from

132 T.N.A., E122/5/7; E122/6/2; A. R. Bridbury, *England and the Salt Trade in the Middle Ages* (Oxford, 1955), pp. 20–1. For salt, see also the references in Rigby, 'Medieval Boston', p. 12. For grain exports, see N. S. B. Gras, *The Evolution of the English Corn Market from the Twelfth to the Eighteenth Century* (New York, 1915), pp. 282–3.

133 Lloyd, *Alien Merchants in England*, p. 52.

134 T.N.A., E122/7/4.

135 T.N.A., E356/9, mm. 24, 34

Nottingham), bowstrings and belts.[136] In particular, by 1390–1, salt had disappeared from alien exports. The English industry had been hit by rising wages in an age of labour shortage and by the flooding of the Lincolnshire turbaries, which provided the industry with its fuel, which meant that it was no longer able to compete with cheaper salt from the Bay of Bourgneuf, south of the Loire estuary.[137] The composition of alien imports had also changed. It was increasingly made up of stockfish, fish oil, furs and other Hanseatic commodities, rather than of goods from the Low Countries, although fur imports were themselves in decline by the end of the century as London came to dominate the trade.[138]

The decline of this branch of alien trade continued throughout the fifteenth century. After 1450, the five-year annual average of the trade was always below £ 1,000, and for most of the first half of the sixteenth century was below £ 500 a year. As late as the 1460s, Hanseatic shipments of stockfish and fish oil from their Bergen *kontor* made up over 90 % of alien miscellaneous imports. Other goods, such as osmund and Spanish iron (which was re-exported from the Low Countries), were of little significance.[139] Given the Hansards' dominance of this branch of Boston's trade, its fluctuations largely reflected the complicated history of Anglo-Hanseatic relations, which involved a series of diplomatic disputes, piracy and even naval warfare. The trade witnessed periodic disastrous slumps, as in 1413–15, when Hansards were arrested in Boston in retaliation for attacks on merchants from Boston in Bergen, after the English seizure of the Hanseatic Bay fleet in 1449 and during the Anglo-Hanseatic warfare of 1468–74. After each slump, the trade revived, but each recovery was smaller and more partial than the last.[140] In the decade from 1475, when the enrolled accounts distinguish the Hanseatic miscellaneous trade from that of other aliens, the Hansards made up around three quarters of the shrunken level of alien imports and exports (see the notes to Figure 6.1), whilst as late as 1491–2 they still accounted for 96 % of such trade.[141]

---

136 See, for instance, T.N.A., E122/7/13; E122/7/22; E122/8/2; E122/8/4; E122/8/7; E122/8/18; E122/212/3.

137 For alien salt imports, see T.N.A., E122/7/22, m. 3d; E122/7/23, m. 2; E122/7/24, m. 1; E122/7/26, m. 1; E122/7/30A, m. 1d.

138 See T.N.A., E122/8/2; E122/8/4; E122/8/27; E122/8/18; Lloyd, *England and the German Hanse*, pp. 82–3; Veale, *English Fur Trade*, p. 71.

139 T.N.A., E122/10/1; E122/10/4; E122/10/7; W. R. Childs, 'England's iron trade in the fifteenth century', *Economic History* Review, 34 (1981), pp. 25–47, at 28–9, 37; Childs, *Anglo-Castilian Trade in the Later Middle Ages*, pp 117, 181.

140 See M. M. Postan, 'The economic and political relations of England and the Hanse from 1400 to 1475', in Power and Postan, *Studies in English Trade in the Fifteenth Century*, pp. 91–153; Lloyd, *England and the German Hanse*, chapters 3–5; Burkhardt, 'One hundred years of thriving commerce at a major English sea port', pp. 70–84; Jenks, *England, die Hanse und Preussen: Handel und Diplomatie*; Rigby, 'Medieval Boston', pp. 23–5.

141 T.N.A., E356/22, mm. 2–4d; E356/23, m. 8.

However, by the early sixteenth century, by which time England's reduced imports of stockfish were shipped mainly from Iceland to London, rather than from Bergen to Boston, merchants from Holland and Zeeland had come to dominate what was left of the alien miscellaneous trade, although the enrolled accounts do note miscellaneous imports and exports by Hansards in 1538–39, 1539–40 and 1546–47 (see the notes to Figure 6.1).[142] Exports of goods such as hemp, mustard-seeds, calf-skins and sea-coal made up less than 5 % of the value of this branch of trade. The miscellaneous alien trade was now mainly comprised of Dutch imports of salted herring, the fifteenth century having seen the development of new methods of fish-curing at sea and the growth of a significant Dutch export trade in salted and barrelled herring. In 1522–23, for instance, herring made up almost 90 % of the value of Boston's alien miscellaneous imports.[143] As we have seen, in the seven years from 1539, alien merchants benefitted from the equalization of their customs rates with those of denizen merchants. The aim of this reduction was to encourage England's commerce, and nationally it does seem to have had a remarkable impact on the volume of alien trade.[144] At Boston, by contrast, any such stimulus was slight. Indeed, the value of the alien miscellaneous trade was actually greater in 1546–7, when aliens were once again paying customs at the previous rates, than in any year since Michaelmas 1539, when they had been exempted from the custom of 3d. in the pound.

Figure 6.1 Total value of alien imports and exports at Boston liable to the custom of 3d. in the pound, 1303–1548.

	£	
10.2.1303–Mich.1303	9365	
Mich.1303–Mich.1304	10698	
Mich.1304–Mich.1305	12819	
Mich.1305–Mich.1306	12876	
Mich.1306–Mich.1307	13646	Note 1
Mich.1307–Mich.1308	12484	
Mich.1308–28.8.1309	11657	
28.8.1309–2.10.1310	No returns	
2.8.1310–Mich.1310	3799	
Mich.1310–27.10.1311	10699	
27.10.1311–20.7.1322	No returns	
20.7.1322–Mich.1323	8193	
Mich.1323–Mich.1324	6548	
Mich.1324–Mich.1325	9018	
Mich.1325–Mich.1326	4014	
Mich.1326–Mich.1327	9520	
Mich.1327–27.8.1328	5050	
Mich.1328–Mich.1329	9705	
Mich.1329–Mich.1330	8686	
Mich,1330–Mich.1331	6588	
Mich.1331–Mich.1332	7249	
Mich.1332–Mich.1333	5295	

142 Lloyd, *England and the German Hanse*, p. 275.

143 T.N.A., E122/12/3 (for 1522–3); E122/12/5; E122/12/8; E122/12/10; R. W. Unger, 'The Netherlands herring fishery in the later Middle Ages: the false legend of William Beukels of Biervliet', *Viator*, 9 (1978), pp. 335–56; N. J. Kerling, *Commercial Relations of Holland and Zeeland with England from the Late Thirteenth Century to the Close of the Middle Ages* (Leiden, 1954), pp. 204, 207.

144 Oldland, *English Woollen Industry*, pp. 66, 278, 311–12.

	£	
Mich.1333–Mich.1334	6565	
Mich.1334–Mich.1335	6924	
Mich.1335–23.8.1336	6968	
23.8.1336–Mich.1337	5922	
Mich.1337–Mich.1338	7010	
Mich.1338–Mich.1339	1846	
Mich.1339–16.7.1340	3737	
16.7.1340–Mich.1341	10062	
Mich.1341–16.6.1342	1684	
16.6.1342–15.7.1343	3232	
15.7.1343–Mich.1351	No returns	
Mich.1351–Mich.1352	2115	
Mich.1352–Mich.1353	3748	
Mich.1353–Mich.1354	6502	Note 2
Mich.1354–Mich.1355	4596	
Mich.1355–Mich.1356	4301	
Mich.1356–Mich.1357	9161	
Mich.1357–Mich.1358	11636	
Mich.1358–Mich.1359	8828	
Mich.1359–Mich.1360	9692	
Mich.1360–Mich.1361	8797	
Mich.1361–Mich.1362	9533	
Mich.1362–Mich.1363	11150	
Mich.1363–2.10.1364	8235	
2.10.1364–20.10.1365	12536	
20.10.1365–Mich.1366	14854	
Mich.1366–Mich.1367	8121	
Mich.1367–Mich.1368	10596	
Mich.1368–Mich.1369	5030	
Mich.1369–Mich.1370	10055	
Mich.1370–Mich.1371	11074	
Mich.1371–Mich.1372	9366	
Mich.1372–24.12.1372	5222	
24.12.1372–26.8.1377	No returns	
26.8.1377–Mich.1378	3397	
Mich.1378–Mich.1379	10341	
Mich.1379–Mich.1380	11363	
Mich.1380–Mich.1381	8763	
Mich.1381–Mich.1382	12678	

	£	
Mich.1382–Mich.1383	7888	
Mich.1383–Mich.1384	6570	
Mich.1384–Mich.1385	12272	
Mich.1385–Mich.1386	6942	
Mich.1386–1.7.1387	6088	
1.7.1387–Mich.1388	8129	
Mich.1388–Mich.1389	10231	
Mich.1389–Mich.1390	7659	
Mich.1390–Mich.1391	5516	
Mich.1391–Mich.1392	7549	
Mich.1392–Mich.1393	6731	
Mich.1393–Mich.1394	4753	
Mich.1394–Mich.1395	6527	
Mich.1395–Mich.1396	7070	
Mich.1396–Mich.1397	6904	
Mich.1397–Mich.1398	4781	
Mich.1398–Mich.1399	7092	
Mich.1399–Mich.1400	5258	
Mich.1400–2.10.1401	8312	
2.10.1401–2.10.1402	6538	
2.10.1402–Mich.1403	6136	
Mich.1403–Mich.1404	4784	
Mich.1404–Mich.1405	4434	
Mich.1405–8.9.1406	6231	
8.9.1406–Mich.1407	6792	
Mich.1407–Mich.1408	3823	
Mich.1408–Mich.1409	4301	
Mich.1409–Mich.1410	4785	
Mich.1410–Mich.1411	4391	
Mich.1411–Mich.1412	3800	
Mich.1412–Mich.1413	5220	
Mich.1413–Mich.1414	350	
Mich.1414–Mich.1415	139	
Mich.1415–Mich.1416	1027	
Mich.1416–Mich.1417	4847	
Mich.1417–Mich.1418	4020	
Mich.1418–Mich.1419	4149	
Mich.1419–10.10.1420	3917	
10.10.1420–Mich.1421	4757	

	£	
Mich.1421–31.8.1422	4068	
1.9.1422–Mich.1423	5874	
Mich.1423–Mich.1424	3227	
Mich.1424–Mich.1425	3309	
Mich.1425–Mich.1426	2645	
Mich.1426–Mich.1427	2515	
Mich.1427–Mich.1428	129	
Mich.1428–1.11.1429	411	
1.11.1429–1.11.1430	155	
1.11.1430–20.10.1431	89	
20.10.1431–Mich.1432	283	
Mich.1432–Mich.1433	230	
Mich.1433–Mich.1434	1264	
Mich.1434–Mich.1435	1098	
Mich.1435–10.10.1436	1147	
10.10.1436–11.11.1437	922	
11.11.1437–Mich.1438	3248	
Mich.1438–Mich.1439	2514	
Mich.1439–Mich.1440	1923	
Mich.1440–30.6.1441	1105	
30.6.1441–Mich.1442	1305	
Mich.1442–12.8.1443	1275	
12.8.1443–12.10.1444	1615	
12.10.1444–12.10.1445	2429	
12.10.1445–24.6.1446	2702	
24.6.1446–18.7.1447	1941	
18.7.1447–21.11.1448	1242	
21.11.1448–21.11.1449	2815	
21.11.1449–Mich.1450	333	
Mich.1450–3.2.1452	227	
3.2.1452–Mich.1452	138	
Mich.1452–Mich.1453	178	
Mich.1453–Mich.1454	9	
Mich.1454–10.10.1455	568	
10.10.1455–10.10.1456	846	
10.10.1456–Mich.1457	1520	
Mich.1457–Mich.1458	1022	
Mich.1458–15.12.1459	No returns	
15.12.1459–1.9.1460	1182	

	£	
1.9.1460–Mich.1461	583	
Mich.1461–Mich.1462	1042	
Mich.1462–20.7.1463	1593	
20.7.1463–3.5.1464	547	
3.5.1464–Mich.1465	736	
Mich.1465–25.3.1466	598	
25.3.1466–25.3.1467	741	
25.3.1467–25.12.1468	680	
25.12.1468–Mich.1469	313	
Mich.1469–13.11.1470	100	Note 3
23.10.1470–Mich.1471	167	Note 4
Mich.1471–8.10.1472	160	Note 5
8.10.1472–8.10.1473	237	
8.10.1473–2.11.1474	444	Note 6
2.11.1474–Mich.1475	673	
Mich.1475–Mich.1476	898	Note 7
Mich.1476–Mich.1477	538	Note 8
Mich.1477–Mich.1478	1100	Note 9
Mich.1478–Mich.1479	597	Note 10
Mich.1479–Mich.1480	439	Note 11
Mich.1480–Mich.1481	535	Note 12
Mich.1481–Mich.1482	948	Note 13
Mich.1482–Mich.1483	794	Note 14
Mich.1483–Mich.1484	354	Note 15
Mich.1484–Mich.1485	586	Note 16
Mich.1485–Mich.1486	76	
Mich.1486–Mich.1487	62	
Mich.1487–Mich.1488	308	
Mich.1488–Mich.1489	395	
Mich.1489–Mich.1490	1243	
Mich.1490–Mich.1491	41	
Mich.1491–Mich.1492	1574	Note 17
Mich.1492–Mich.1493	35	
Mich.1493–Mich.1494	51	Note 18
Mich.1494–Mich.1495	50	
Mich.1495–Mich.1496–	42	
Mich.1496–Mich.1497	270	
Mich.1497–Mich.1498	160	
Mich.1498–Mich.1499	63	Note 19

	£	
Mich.1499–Mich.1500	114	
Mich.1500–Mich.1501	131	
Mich.1501–Mich.1502	325	
Mich.1502–Mich.1503	433	
Mich.1503–Mich.1504	701	
Mich.1504–Mich.1505	162	
Mich.1505–Mich.1506	168	
Mich.1506–Mich.1507	313	
Mich.1507–Mich.1508	316	
Mich.1508–Mich.1509	147	
Mich.1509–Mich.1510	250	
Mich.1510–Mich.1511	113	
Mich.1511–Mich.1512	268	
Mich.1512–Mich.1513	1	
Mich.1513–Mich.1514	169	
Mich.1514–Mich.1515	353	
Mich.1515–Mich.1516	363	
Mich.1516–Mich.1517	83	
Mich.1517–Mich.1518	391	
Mich.1518–Mich.1519	383	
Mich.1519–Mich.1520	454	
Mich.1520–Mich.1521	280	
Mich.1521–Mich.1522	0	
Mich.1522–Mich.1523	208	
Mich.1523–Mich.1524	45	

	£	
Mich.1524–Mich.1525	211	
Mich.1525–Mich.1526	258	
Mich.1526–Mich.1527	223	
Mich.1527–Mich.1528	234	
Mich.1528–Mich.1529	218	
Mich.1529–Mich.1530	330	
Mich.1530–Mich.1531	129	
Mich.1531–Mich.1532	283	
Mich.1532–Mich.1533	0	
Mich.1533–Mich.1534	87	
Mich.1534–Mich.1535	224	
Mich.1535–Mich.1536	217	
Mich.1536–Mich.1537	228	
Mich.1537–Mich.1538	204	
Mich.1538–Mich.1539	1339	Note 20
Mich.1539–Mich.1540	726	Note 21
Mich.1540–Mich.1541	596	
Mich.1541–Mich.1542	531	
Mich.1542–Mich.1543	207	
Mich.1543–Mich.1544	145	
Mich.1544–Mich.1545	415	
Mich.1545–Mich.1546	0	
Mich.1546–Mich.1547	835	Note 22
Mich.1547–Mich.1548	385	

(Source: T.N.A., E356 Enrolled customs accounts)

Notes to Figure 6.1:

- Note 1. The enrolled account wrongly gives a customs payment of £ 19 4s. 5½d. for alien miscellaneous imports, but this should read £ 119 4s. 5½d. (T.N.A., E356/2, m. 28d.).
- Note 2. The enrolled account from Michaelmas 1354 to 29 January 1355 notes the customs paid on alien miscellaneous imports 'at Boston and London', but the London account for this period makes no mention of Boston (T.N.A., E356/9, mm. 24, 34).
- Note 3. Dates as given in the enrolled account.
- Note 4. Dates as given in the enrolled account.
- Note 5. £ 160 9s. 8d. of imports and exports, including £ 18 by merchants of Veere.
- Note 6. £ 444 9s. 2d. of imports and exports, including £ 442 5s. 10d. by merchants of Veere.

- Note 7. £ 898 7s. 8d. of imports and exports, including £ 169 13s. 4d. by merchants of Veere and £ 435 11s. 8d. by Hansards.
- Note 8. £ 537 15s. 5d. of imports and exports, including £ 389 9s. 4d. by merchants of Veere.
- Note 9. £ 1099 15s. 6d of imports and exports, including £ 681 4s. by Hansards.
- Note 10. £ 579 of imports and exports, including £ 144 15s. 8d. by merchants of Veere and £ 377 0s. 2d. by Hansards.
- Note 11. £ 438 11s. 8d. of imports and exports, including £ 414 10s. by Hansards.
- Note 12. £ 535 3s. 10d. of imports and exports, including £ 416 15s. by Hansards.
- Note 13. £ 948 5s. 4d. of imports and exports, including £ 816 6s. 8d. by Hansards.
- Note 14. £ 793 12s. 8d. of imports and exports, including £ 546 by Hansards.
- Note 15. £ 353 19s. of imports and exports, including £ 210 10s by Hansards.
- Note 16. £ 585 15s. of imports and exports, including £ 457 13s. 4d. by Hansards.
- Note 17. £ 1574 6s. 8d. of imports and exports, including £ 1512 by Hansards.
- Note 18. £ 51 of imports and exports, including £ 41 13s. 4d by a Hansard.
- Note 19. £ 62 13s. 4d. of imports and exports, including £ 27 10s. by a Hansard.
- Note 20. £ 1338 11s. 4d. of imports and exports, including £ 424 by Hansards.
- Note 21. £ 726 7s. 8d. of imports and exports, including £ 34 6s. 8d by Hansards.
- Note 22. The imports and exports paying the customs of 3d. in the pound in this year are said to be by Hansards and aliens.

Figure 6.2 Total value of alien imports and exports at Boston liable to the custom of 3d. in the pound, 1303–1548.

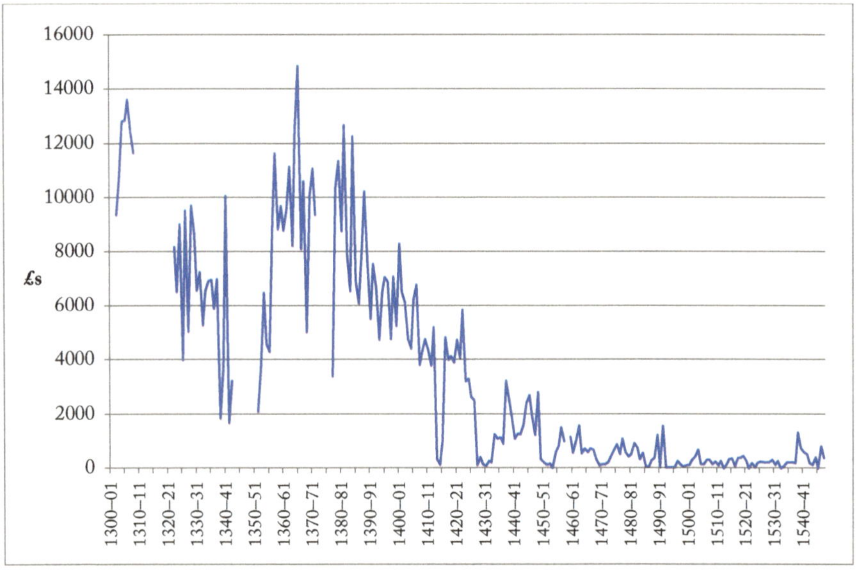

Figure 6.3 The balance of trade in alien imports and exports at Boston liable to the custom of 3d. in the pound, 1303–1335.

	Imports	Exports	Imports as % of total
10.2.1303–Mich.1303	5319	4045	57
Mich.1303–Mich.1304	8201	2497	77
Mich.1304–Mich.1305	8785	4035	69
Mich.1305–Mich.1306	9172	3704	71
Mich.1306–Mich.1307	9538	4108	70
Mich.1307–Mich.1308	8667	3817	69
Mich.1308–28.8.1309	9958	1699	85
28.8.1309–2.8.1310	No returns		
2.8.1310–Mich.1310	2661	1118	70
Mich.1310–27.10.1311	7515	3813	66
27.10.1311–20.7.1322	No returns		
20.7.1322–Mich.1323	6601	1592	81
Mich.1323–Mich.1324	5955	593	91
Mich.1324–Mich.1325	7557	1461	84
Mich.1325–Mich.1326	3264	749	81
Mich.1326–Mich.1327	8035	1685	89
Mich.1327–27.8.1328	4294	755	85
27.8.1328–Mich.1329	8170	1536	84
Mich.1329–Mich.1330	7467	1219	84
Mich.1330–Mich.1331	5684	904	86
Mich.1331–Mich.1332	6223	1026	86
Mich.1332–Mich.1333	4926	369	93
Mich.1333–Mich.1334	5329	1235	81
Mich.1334–28.4.1335	2242	483	82

(Source: T.N.A., E356, Enrolled customs accounts)

2.7 Alien and denizen woollen and worsted exports, 1353–1548

In 1347 a comprehensive new set of customs was imposed on England's growing cloth export trade. Since the ancient custom of 1275 and the new custom of 1303 on wool, woolfells and were known as the 'great custom', the 1303 new custom on cloth, wax and miscellaneous goods and the cloth custom of 1347 together came to be known as the 'petty customs'.[145] At Boston, the same pair of collectors normally

145 Gras, *Early English Customs System*, p. 435.

accounted for both the great and the petty customs, although occasionally, as in 1390–91 and 1397–98, responsibility for these two customs was divided between three different collectors.[146] Denizen merchants had not been liable to the custom on cloth exports introduced as part of the 1303 new custom, but from 1347 they paid a duty on their exports of 1s. 2d. per cloth of assize without grain, 1s. 9d. per cloth partly in grain, and 2s. 4d. per cloth in grain. The 1347 custom also included new charges on alien cloth exports, which were now charged at the rate of 1s. 9d. per cloth without grain, 2s. 7d. per cloth partly in grain, and 3s. 6d. per cloth in grain.[147] The 1347 custom also included specific duties on the export of worsteds (see below). There was some initial confusion as to whether non-Hanseatic aliens were liable to both the 1303 and the 1347 duties. At first, these aliens seem only to have paid the 1347 duty on their cloth exports from Boston. From 1361, this remained the case in all of England's ports with the exception of London, where aliens were required to pay both duties.[148] Eventually, however, from Michaelmas 1381, the London practice was applied nationally and non-Hanseatic aliens in Boston, as in other ports, were required to pay both the 1303 and the 1347 customs on their cloth exports.[149]

Cloth exports by Hanseatic merchants were treated differently from both those by denizens and those by other aliens. The enrolled accounts for the years between 1351 and 1361 do not distinguish cloth exports by the Hansards from those of other aliens, and indicate that all alien cloth exports in this period were charged only with the 1347 cloth custom rather than with the customs on cloth exports introduced in 1303. It therefore appears that the Hansards, like other aliens, did pay the 1347 cloth custom in this decade, even though they were later to claim exemption from it.[150] Indeed, in May 1358 and again in the following October, the Hansards explicitly acknowledged that they were liable to the 1347 custom on their cloth exports. At this time their complaint was only that their cloth exports were being charged with both the 1347 and the 1303 customs in Boston, and that their exports of narrow cloths and smaller pieces of cloth were being charged at the 1347 rate for cloths of assize or half-cloths, even though they had traditionally paid the *ad valorem* duty of 3d. in the pound on such non-standard cloths.[151] Yet, despite this admission of liability to the 1347 custom, the Hansards were soon arguing that their cloth exports should only pay the 1303 custom rather than the higher rates introduced in 1347, claiming that Edward I's *Carta Mercatoria* and the privileges granted to them by Edward II in 1317 protected them against the imposition of

146 Rigby, *The Overseas Trade of Boston*, p. 221.
147 Gras, *Early English Customs System*, p. 72; Jenks, *Enrolled Customs Accounts*, Part 3, pp. v–vi.
148 T.N.A., E356/7; E356/9; Lloyd, *England and the German Hanse*, pp. 32–3.
149 T.N.A., E356/14, m. 11d.; Lloyd, *England and the German Hanse*, p. 33.
150 T.N.A., E356/7, mm. 7d.-10; E356/9, mm. 24–24d.
151 *Calendar of Close Rolls, 1354–60*, pp. 448, 467, 518.

any further customs. Their claim was successful, and so from 8 February 1361 the Boston customs accounts distinguish cloth exports by Hansards, who paid only at the 1303 rates (e.g. 1s. per cloth without grain, which made up the vast bulk of exports), from those of denizens, who paid only at the 1347 rates (i.e. 1s. 2d. per cloth without grain), and from those by non-Hanseatic aliens, who paid only the 1347 custom before 1381 (i.e. 1s. 9d. per cloth without grain) and who were charged with both the 1303 and 1347 customs thereafter (i.e. 2s. 9d. per cloth without grain).[152]

Another group of merchants whose cloth exports are distinguished in the enrolled accounts are the merchants of Veere, who, as part of the privileges granted them by Edward IV noted above, had only to pay a custom of 1s. per cloth exported (i.e. the 1303 rate) from 1471 to 1483.[153] Their exports are given in the notes to Figure 7.1, below. As we have seen (in section 2.6, above), from 6 April 1539 there was an experimental seven-year period when denizen and alien customs rates were equalized, but, fortunately for our purposes, the enrolled accounts continue to provide separate totals for cloth exports by alien and denizen merchants, allowing us to distinguish their trade during these years.[154]

No separate returns for the 1347 cloth custom survive for Boston from 1347 to 1353, during which time the royal butler accounted at the Exchequer for the custom for all England's ports together.[155] Figures 7.1 and 7.2 trace the fluctuations in cloth exports by denizen, alien and Hanseatic merchants from Boston between 1353 and 1548, with the exception of the period from December 1372 and August 1377 when the custom was farmed.[156] Unlike the early fourteenth century, nearly all of Boston's cloth exports after 1353 were for cloths without grain, (with England's few surviving exports of scarlets and cloths in grain now being shipped via London). The totals in Figure 7.1 thus include the extremely small amounts of cloths in grain or partly in grain which were exported there.[157] A complication occurred in the five years from 1367, when the enrolled accounts include cloths said to have been 'imported or exported' by denizen and alien merchants at the rate of 1s. per cloth. Since, in theory, denizen merchants were not liable to a custom of 1s. per cloth and were not supposed to pay customs on their cloth imports, it is

152 T.N.A., E356/7, m. 10; *Calendar of Close Rolls, 1360–64*, p. 152; Lloyd, *England and the German Hanse*, pp. 33–4; Jenks, *Enrolled Customs Accounts*, Part 3, p. vi.

153 See footnote 123, above.

154 TN.A., E356/27, mm. 4–6.

155 Jenks, *Enrolled Customs Accounts*, Part 3, pp. 625–7. It is thus misleading to say that there were 'no recorded shipments' of cloth from Boston in this period (Rigby, 'Medieval Boston', p. 17).

156 Some of these figures differ from those in Carus-Wilson and Coleman, *England's Export Trade*, but such differences are usually slight and generally result from the way in which totals have been rounded up or down to the nearest cloth.

157 Childs, 'The English export trade in cloth', p. 139.

tempting to regard this as a scribal error and to suppose that these cloths belonged only to Hanseatic merchants, who, as we saw above, had paid cloth custom at this rate since 1361.[158] Yet, in fact, the account for 1371–2 clearly distinguishes 41 cloths exported by denizen merchants at the rate of 1s. per cloth from both the 1,500 cloths exported which were charged at the standard denizen rate of 1s. 2d. per cloth, and the 1,625 cloths exported by Hansards at their standard rate of 1s. per cloth (see Figure 7.1, note 7, below).[159] It is not clear why denizen merchants were charged at two different rates, or why they should have been liable to a custom of 1s. per cloth.[160] In order to arrive at a figure for total cloth exports, cloths said to have been imported or exported in this period by aliens and denizens at 1s. per cloth are included in the total for Hanseatic exports in Figure 7.1, although this may slightly inflate this total.

As is well known, England's exports of woollen cloth boomed in the second half of the fourteenth century, particularly in the late 1360s and again in the late 1380s, as the domestic industry came to enjoy the protection afforded by embargoes on alien cloth imports and by the heavy subsidies imposed by the Crown on English wool exports, which raised the costs of foreign clothmakers.[161] Boston shared in this boom, with exports in the combined customs jurisdictions of Boston and Lynn rising from around 650 cloths a year in the period from 1353 to 1362 to almost 3,000 a year from 1363 to 1372, although, as the notes to Figure 7.1 indicate, the figure for the latter period may be inflated by the inclusion of some imports. The farming of the Lynn customs after 1377 means that we do not have figures for that port's cloth exports in this period, and thus it is difficult to estimate the proportion of cloth that was shipped through Boston itself after the two customs jurisdictions were merged in 1353. Nevertheless, Boston's cloth exports were certainly growing in the second half of the century, rising from an annual average of around 650 cloths in Boston and Lynn between 1353 and 1362, to 2,400–2,800 cloths a year in Boston alone from 1377 to 1407. Unlike other east coast provincial ports, where denizen merchants dominated the cloth trade, the bulk of these exports was undertaken by Hanseatic merchants, particularly those of Lübeck, who accounted for around three quarters of the trade when it was at its peak in the final decade of the fourteenth century. Indeed, before the 1390s, Hanseatic cloth exports from Boston exceeded even those from London. However, Boston's pre-eminence in

158 T.N.A., E356/7, mm.13–14.

159 T.N.A., E356/7, m. 14.

160 Carus-Wilson and Coleman claim that the account for 1371–72 includes 1,625 cloths imported and exported by denizen and alien merchants (*England's Export Trade*, p. 79), like those in the accounts for 1368–71, but the 1371–2 account actually distinguishes the 1,625 cloths exported by Hansards from the 41 cloths which were exported by denizens at the rate of 1s. per cloth.

161 J. S. Lee, *The Medieval Clothier* (Woodbridge, 2018), pp. 8–16; Oldland, *English Woollen Industry*, pp. 60, 113, 115, 131–2, 154, 200–1.

the trade may be exaggerated by the practice of charging non-standard cloths with the *ad valorem* custom of 3d. in the pound, rather than with the customs on standard cloths of assize, because the trade in non-standard cloths was of greater significance in London than it was in Boston.[162] Exports by other aliens at Boston were insignificant, usually consisting of fewer than 50 cloths a year in the 1390s, with denizens accounting for the remaining 600 or so cloths, the bulk of the latter probably being shipped to the Baltic, where denizen merchants were now making great inroads.[163] The sources of the cloth exported from Boston are, of course, not given in the customs accounts, but the port probably benefitted from the revival of Lincoln's textile industry from the 1340s to around 1380 (although the city no longer specialised in expensive scarlets). Boston's trade was also stimulated by the emergence of Coventry as one of the leading clothmaking centres in the country in the late fourteenth and early fifteenth centuries.[164]

The fifteenth century saw a steady decline in Boston's cloth exports: from almost 3,000 cloths a year in the 1390s, the trade had fallen to around 2,000 cloths a year in the 1420s, to fewer than 600 cloths a year by the 1460s and to under 100 cloths a year from the 1490s. Given the continuing domination of Boston's cloth exports by Hanseatic merchants, the trade's fluctuations were largely determined by the troubled state of Anglo–Hanseatic relations (see section 2.6, above). After the Treaty of Utrecht of 1474 and the resolution of Anglo–Hanseatic differences to the satisfaction of the Hanse, the Hansards' cloth exports from England, like those of the cloth trade in general, which trebled in volume between the 1460s and 1540s, reached new peaks.[165] Yet, whilst the Hansards' trade from London boomed, particularly that to Cologne and Frankfurt rather than to the Baltic, their cloth exports from Boston enjoyed only a brief recovery. By 1481 the Hanseatic warehouse in the port was said to be 'dilapidated'.[166] Hanseatic cloth exports from Boston ceased after 1502, despite the efforts made in 1505 by Lady Margaret Beaufort, the owner of the main manor in Boston, to lure the Hansards back to the port by the

162 Carus-Wilson and Coleman, *England's Export Trade*, pp. 80–4; Lloyd, *England and the German Hanse*, pp. 70, 75, 93, 97, 368; Burkhardt, 'One hundred years of thriving commerce at a major English sea port', pp. 67–8, 70.

163 Lloyd, *England and the German Hanse*, pp. 85, 166–8; S. Jenks, 'Trade and relations between Lynn and the Hanse in the Middle Ages', in K. Friedland and P. Richards, eds, *Essays in Hanseatic History: The King's Lynn Symposium, 1998* (Dereham, 2005), pp. 94–114, at 100–101; J. Sarnowsky, 'The "Golden Age" of the Hanseatic League', in Harreld, *A Companion to the Hanseatic League*, pp. 64–100, at 82–3; Rigby, 'Medieval Boston', p. 17.

164 Kissane, *Civic Community in Medieval Lincoln*, pp. 24–6; Rigby, 'Medieval Boston', pp. 16–17; Oldland, *English Woollen Industry*, pp. 122, 124–5, 142, 181–2.

165 Oldland, *English Woollen Industry*, pp. 267–8, 276–7; Burkhardt, 'One hundred years of thriving commerce at a major English sea port', pp. 70–84.

166 Carus-Wilson and Coleman, *England's Export Trade*, pp. 138–9; Nedkvitne, *The German Hansa and Bergen*, p. 153.

offer of favourable treatment. Lynn was more successful than Boston in holding on to what little was left of the Hanse's trade in the ports of the Wash.[167]

Denizen merchants were sometimes able to take short-term advantage of disruptions to the trade of the Hanse, as they did in 1428–30, a time of conflict between the Hanseatic League and Denmark, when Hanseatic exports at Boston collapsed and denizen exports reached an all-time high of over 1,600 cloths a year. Yet, in the long run, neither denizen nor non-Hanseatic alien cloth exports took the place of those by the Hansards; from the 1480s, denizens were exporting fewer than 100 cloths a year from Boston, with exports by other aliens being even less significant. By the 1540s, cloth exports had virtually disappeared from Boston, even though such exports were booming nationally.[168] Nationally, the reduction of the cloth custom paid by aliens from 2s. 9d. to 1s. 2d. as part of the equalization of alien and denizen custom rates in the years between 1539 and 1546 (see section 2.6, above) encouraged exports of English cloth by alien merchants. At Boston, however, their trade remained minimal.[169] By this date, England's cloth exports were almost entirely shipped via London. Whereas in the mid-fifteenth century, London had shipped less than half of England's cloth exports, a century later it was responsible for about 90 % of the trade, which was mainly sent from to the great international entrepôt of Antwerp and to the fairs of Bergen-op-Zoom.[170] The capital had increased its trade even at the expense of Bristol and Hull, ports much better placed than Boston to take advantage of the West Country and West Riding centres of cloth production. Coventry's cloth could be exported as easily from London as via Boston whilst the clothiers of Suffolk, England's leading textile region by 1500, also marketed their output via the capital.[171]

---

167 Lloyd, *England and the German Hanse*, p. 277; Fudge, *Cargoes, Embargoes and Emissaries*, p. 157; Nedkvitne, *The German Hansa and Bergen*, pp. 153–4. For Beaufort's efforts to reverse Boston's commercial decline, see M. K. Jones and M. G. Underwood, *The King's Mother: Lady Margaret Beaufort, Countess of Richmond and Derby* (Cambridge, 1992), pp. 128–30.

168 Oldland, *English Woollen Industry*, p. 192, 219, 267–8, 276.

169 T.N.A., E356/27, mm. 4–6; Lloyd, *England and the German Hanse*, pp. 270–1; Oldland, *English Woollen Industry*, p. 278.

170 D. C. Coleman, *The Economy of England, 1450–1750* (London, 1977), pp. 49–54; F. J. Fisher, 'Commercial trends and policy in sixteenth-century England', *Economic History Review*, 10 (1940), pp. 95–117, at 96–8; Oldland, *English Woollen Industry*, pp 12, 134, 202, 254–6, 262, 268.

171 For references to the rise of London see Rigby, 'Medieval Boston', pp. 25–6. See also J. R. Oldland, 'London's trade in the time of Richard III', *The Ricardian*, 24 (2014), pp. 1–30; J. R. Oldland, 'The expansion of London's overseas trade from 1475 to 1520', in C. M. Barron and A. F. Sutton, eds, *The Medieval Merchant: Proceedings of the 2012 Harlaxton Symposium* (Donington, 2014), pp. 55–92; N. R. Amor, *From Wool to Cloth: The Triumph of the Suffolk Clothier* (Bungay, 2016), pp. 201–6, 216–7; C. M. Barron, *London in the Later Middle Ages: Government and People, 1200–1500* (Oxford, 2004), pp. 101–17; Oldland, *English Woollen Industry*, pp. 278–9.

Figure 7.1 Cloth exports from Boston, 1353–1548.

	Denizens	All aliens	Hanse	Non-Hanse Aliens	Total	
20.4.1347–30.7.1353	No returns					
30.7.1353–Mich.1354	189	85			274	
Mich.1354–Mich.1355	104	27			131	
Mich.1355–Mich.1356	79	22			101	
Mich.1356–30.9.1357	299	462			761	
30.9.1357–Mich.1358	438	561			999	
Mich.1358–Mich.1359	529	462			991	
Mich.1359–Mich.1360	474	550			1024	
Mich.1360–Mich.1361	604		80	196	880	Note 1
Mich.1361–Mich.1362	474		145	98	717	
Mich.1362–18.2.1363	No returns					
18.2.1363–Mich.1363	43		74	847	964	
Mich.1363–2.10.1364	505		1783	175	2463	
2.10.1364–20.10.1365	674		1766	282	2722	
20.10.1365–Mich.1366	729		1975	71	2775	Note 2
Mich.1366–Mich.1367	1047		1197	62	2306	Note 3
Mich.1367–Mich.1368	1140		2009	47	3106	Note 4
Mich.1368–Mich.1369	1455		929	65	2449	Note 5
Mich.1369–Mich.1370	2308		1074	122	3504	Note 6
Mich.1370–Mich.1371	1541		1646	84	3271	Note 7
Mich.1371–Mich.1372	1541		1625	129	3295	Note 8
Mich.1372–24.12.1372	80		76	6	162	
24.12.1372–26.8.1377	No returns					
26.8.1377–Mich.1378	508		1079	15	1602	
Mich.1378–Mich.1379	536		0	1423	1959	Note 9
Mich.1379–Mich.1380	542		2113	34	2689	
Mich.1380–Mich.1381	668		1850	19	2537	
Mich.1381–Mich.1382	959		1879	13	2851	
Mich.1382–Mich.1383	680		1094	7	1781	
Mich.1383–Mich.1384	968		1023	18	2009	
Mich.1384–Mich.1385	343		2537	16	2896	
Mich.1385–Mich.1386	903		2014	47	2964	
Mich.1386–26.11.1387	1053		2060	12	3125	
26.11.1387–Mich.1388	532		1926	22	2480	
Mich.1388–Mich.1389	803		2159	9	2971	
Mich.1389–Mich.1390	1056		1824	41	2921	Note 10
Mich.1390–Mich.1391	1029		1708	11	2748	

	Denizens	All aliens	Hanse	Non-Hanse Aliens	Total	
Mich.1391–Mich.1392	596		2550	14	3160	Note 11
Mich.1392–Mich.1393	175		1943	6	2124	
Mich.1393–Mich.1394	314		2107	64	2485	
Mich.1394–Mich.1395	504		2209	43	2756	
Mich.1395–Mich.1396	498		2524	26	3048	
Mich.1396–Mich.1397	578		2634	18	3230	
Mich.1397–Mich.1398	801		2059	17	2877	
Mich.1398–Mich.1399	590		2580	16	3186	
Mich.1399–Mich.1400	680		1891	12	2583	
Mich.1400–2.10.1401	936		2089	10	3035	
2.10.1401–2.10.1402	834		2934	13	3781	
2.10.1402–Mich.1403	830		1808	28	2666	
Mich.1403–Mich.1404	160		1533	9	1702	
Mich.1404–Mich.1405	277		1643	5	1925	
Mich.1405–8.9.1406	409		1368	4	1781	
8.9.1406–Mich.1407	300		1812	3	2115	
Mich.1407–Mich.1408	324		1452	32	1808	
Mich.1408–Mich.1409	462		1419	40	1921	
Mich.1409–Mich.1410	276		1315	13	1604	
Mich.1410–Mich.1411	236		1004	10	1250	
Mich.1411–Mich.1412	144		1041	2	1187	
Mich.1412–Mich.1413	184		1793	3	1980	
Mich.1413–Mich.1414	525		95	25	645	
Mich.1414–Mich.1415	246		12	5	263	
Mich.1415–Mich.1416	311		348	9	668	
Mich.1416–Mich.1417	55		1481	9	1545	
Mich.1417–Mich.1418	335		1461	36	1832	
Mich.1418–Mich.1419	314		1484	15	1813	
Mich.1419–10.10.1420	348		1882	38	2268	
10.10.1420–Mich.1421	481		2179	20	2680	
Mich.1421–31.8.1422	233		2410	6	2649	
1.9.1422–Mich.1423	497		1643	20	2160	
Mich.1423–Mich.1424	772		2151	18	941	
Mich.1424–Mich.1425	809		1801	17	2627	
Mich.1425–Mich.1426	606		1463	12	2081	
Mich.1426–Mich.1427	585		1051	8	1644	
Mich.1427–Mich.1428	831		0	5	836	
Mich.1428–1.11.1429	1686		3	57	1746	
1.11.1429–1.11.1430	1651		17	32	1700	

	Denizens	All aliens	Hanse	Non-Hanse Aliens	Total	
1.11.1430–20.10.1431	384		0	30	414	
20.10.1431–Mich.1432	697		41	13	751	
Mich.1432–Mich.1433	394		47	12	453	
Mich.1433–Mich.1434	507		521	2	1028	
Mich.1434–Mich.1435	651		593	0	1244	
Mich.1435–10.10.1436	96		3	0	99	
10.10.1436–11.11.1437	394		1176	21	1591	
11.11.1437–Mich.1438	396		1393	33	1822	
Mich.1438–Mich.1439	376		1197	44	1617	
Mich.1439–Mich.1440	343		915	0	1258	
Mich.1440–31.6.1441	142		53	0	195	
31.6.1441–Mich.1442	277		836	5	1118	
Mich.1442–12.8.1443	203		890	1	1094	
12.8.1443–12.10.1444	360		957	23	1340	
12.10.1444–12.10.1445	351		1249	4	1604	
12.10.1445–24.6.1446	339		753	10	1102	
24.6.1446–18.7.1447	382		1164	1	1547	
18.7.1447–21.11.1448	465		506	5	976	
21.11.1448–21.11.1449	102		1463	2	1567	
21.11.1449–Mich.1450	465		101	31	599	
Mich.1450–3.2.1452	499		0	12	511	
3.2.1452–Mich.1452	239		0	2	241	
Mich.1452–Mich.1453	53		0	13	66	
Mich.1453–Mich.1454	317		0	2	319	
Mich.1454–10.10.1455	207		138	0	345	
10.10.1455–19.10.1456	91		536	1	628	
19.10.1456–Mich.1457	185		81	52	318	
Mich.1457–Mich.1458	5		112	0	117	
Mich.1458–15.12.1459	No returns					
15.12.1459–1.9.1460	55		948	3	1006	
1.9.1460–Mich.1461	188		346	3	537	
Mich.1461–Mich.1462	135		636	0	771	
Mich.1462–20.7.1463	189		0	0	189	
20.7.1463–2.5.1465	278		279	9	566	
2.5.1465–Mich.1465	54		450	4	508	
Mich.1465–25.3.1467	387		95	144	626	Note 12
25.3.1467–6.3.1468	185		42	1	228	
6.3.1468–25.12.1468	576		56	1	633	
25.12.1468–Mich.1469	497		0	5	502	

	Denizens	All aliens	Hanse	Non-Hanse Aliens	Total	
Mich.1469–13.11.1470	622		0	4	626	
26.10.1470–Mich.1471	273		0	30	303	Note 13
Mich.1471–8.10.1472	372		0	43	415	
8.10.1472–8.10.1473	479		0	150	629	Note 14
8.10.1473–2.11.1474	337		0	206	543	Note 15
2.11.1474–Mich.1475	169		31	170	370	Note 16
Mich.1475–Mich.1476	12		283	5	400	Note 17
Mich.1476–Mich.1477	84		0	6	90	Note 18
Mich.1477–Mich.1478	107		548	7	662	Note 19
Mich.1478–Mich.1479	204		195	21	420	Note 20
Mich.1479–Mich.1480	68		265	0	333	
Mich.1480–Mich.1481	41		242	0	283	
Mich.1481–Mich.1482	152		62	8	222	Note 21
Mich.1482–Mich.1483	54		214	55	323	Note 22
Mich.1483–Mich.1484	66		152	0	218	
Mich.1484–Mich.1485	54		283	0	337	
Mich.1485–Mich.1486	51		0	0	51	
Mich.1486–Mich.1487	99		0	0	99	
Mich.1487–Mich.1488	88		67	0	155	
Mich.1488–Mich.1489	30		32	0	62	
Mich.1489–Mich.1490	90		31	0	121	
Mich.1490–Mich.1491	50		0	0	50	
Mich.1491–Mich.1492	9		146	0	155	
Mich.1492–Mich.1493	38		0	0	38	
Mich.1493–Mich.1494	53		0	0	53	
Mich.1494–Mich.1495	82		5	0	87	
Mich.1495–Mich.1496	50		0	0	50	
Mich.1496–Mich.1497	22		15	18	55	
Mich.1497–Mich.1498	71		0	0	71	
Mich.1498–Mich.1499	42		1	0	43	
Mich.1499–Mich.1500	56		7	8	71	
Mich.1500–Mich.1501	123		0	7	130	
Mich.1501–Mich.1502	103		6	7	116	
Mich.1502–Mich.1503	54		0	7	61	
Mich.1503–Mich.1504	6		0	11	17	
Mich.1504–Mich.1505	11		11	0	22	
Mich.1505–Mich.1506	9		0	29	38	
Mich.1506–Mich.1507	25		0	59	84	
Mich.1507–Mich.1508	28		0	24	52	

	Denizens	All aliens	Hanse	Non-Hanse Aliens	Total	
Mich.1508–Mich.1509	5		0	3	8	
Mich.1509–Mich.1510	11		0	4	15	
Mich.1510–Mich.1511	24		0	0	24	
Mich.1511–Mich.1512	3		0	3	6	
Mich.1512–Mich.1513	10		0	2	12	
Mich.1513–Mich.1514	5		0	4	9	
Mich.1514–Mich.1515	26		0	4	30	
Mich.1515–Mich.1516	6		0	13	19	
Mich.1516–Mich.1517	2		0	8	10	
Mich.1517–Mich.1518	2		46	16	64	
Mich.1518–Mich.1519	31		0	16	47	
Mich.1519–Mich.1520	3		0	19	22	
Mich.1520–Mich.1521	8		0	1	9	
Mich.1521–Mich.1522	0		0	0	0	
Mich.1522–Mich.1523	2		0	0	2	
Mich.1523–Mich.1524	12		0	0	12	
Mich.1524–Mich.1525	13		0	7	20	
Mich.1525–Mich.1526	10		0	3	22	
Mich.1526–Mich.1527	16		0	4	20	
Mich.1527–Mich.1528	4		0	4	8	
Mich.1528–Mich.1529	8		0	9	17	
Mich.1529–Mich.1530	10		0	12	22	
Mich.1530–Mich.1531	13		0	7	20	
Mich.1531–Mich.1532	7		0	1	8	
Mich.1532–Mich.1533	35		0	0	35	
Mich.1533–Mich.1534	61		0	0	61	
Mich.1534–Mich.1535	55		0	28	83	
Mich.1535–Mich.1536	38		0	8	46	
Mich.1536–Mich.1537	53		0	0	53	
Mich.1537–Mich.1538	17		0	0	17	
Mich.1538–Mich.1539	6		0	14	20	
Mich.1539–Mich.1540	4		0	12	16	
Mich.1540–Mich.1541	2		0	3	5	
Mich.1541–Mich.1542	10		0	13	23	
Mich.1542–Mich.1543	0		0	3	3	
Mich.1543–Mich.1544	0		0	0	0	
Mich.1544–Mich.1545	0		0	4	4	
Mich.1545–Mich.1546	0		0	0	0	
Mich.1546–Mich.1547	0		0	0	0	

	Denizens	All aliens	Hanse	Non-Hanse Aliens	Total
Mich.1547–Mich.1548	0		0	0	0

(Source: T.N.A., E356 Enrolled customs accounts)

Notes to Figure 7.1:

- Note 1. Hanseatic exports are distinguished from 8 February 1361 (T.N.A., E356/7, m. 10d.)
- Note 2. In addition to non-Hanseatic alien exports charged at 1s. 9d. per cloth, the account for 1365–6 also includes 1,974¾ cloths (rounded up here to 1,975) which are said to have been imported and exported by 'alien' merchants at the rate of 1s. per cloth as normally paid by Hanseatic merchants. Since no Hanseatic cloths are distinguished in this account, it seems likely that these were Hanseatic cloths paying custom at the 1303 new custom rate for cloth imports and exports (T.N.A., E356/7, m. 12), and so they have been included here in the column for Hanseatic cloths.
- Note 3. In addition to the 1,197 cloths exported by Hansards, the account for 1366–7 also includes 118 cloths imported by 'aliens' paying custom at 1s. per cloth (T.N.A., E356/7, m. 12d), the rate paid by aliens (whether Hanseatic or not) for cloth imports under the 1303 new custom. These 118 cloths are not included in the totals here.
- Note 4. In addition to the denizen cloths customed at 1s. 2d. per cloth and the non-Hanseatic alien cloths customed at 1s. 9d. per cloth, the account for 1367–68 also includes 2,009 cloths said to have been imported and exported by denizen and alien merchants at the rate of 1s. per cloth (T.N.A., E356/7, m. 13). The 2,009 cloths are listed here in the column for Hanseatic cloths for 1367–8.
- Note 5. The account for 1368–69 includes 929 cloths which are said to have been imported and exported by denizen and alien merchants at the rate of 1s. per cloth (T.N.A., E356/7, m.13; see note 3, above). They are listed here in the column for Hanseatic cloths.
- Note 6. The account for 1369–70 includes 1,074 cloths which are said to have been imported and exported by denizen and alien merchants at the rate of 1s. per cloth (T.N.A., E356/7, m.13d., see note 3, above). They are listed here in the column for Hanseatic cloths.
- Note 7. The account for 1370–71 includes 1,646 cloths which are said to have been imported and exported by denizen and alien merchants at the rate of 1s. per cloth (T.N.A., E356/7, m.14, see note 3, above). They are listed here in the column for Hanseatic cloths.
- Note 8. The account for 1371–72 explicitly distinguishes four rates of custom: 41 cloths exported by denizens at the rate of 1s. per cloth, even though in theory denizens were supposed to pay 1s. 2d. per cloth (see note 3 above); 1,500 cloths exported by denizens at the standard rate of 1s. 2d. per cloth; 129 cloths exported

by non-Hanseatic merchants at their standard rate of 1s. 9d. per cloth; and 1,625 cloths exported by Hanseatic merchants at their standard rate of 1s. per cloth (T.N.A., E356/7, m. 14).

- Note 9. The account for 1378–79 does not include any cloth exports charged with the 1s. per cloth usually paid by Hansards, but it is likely that Hanseatic cloths made up the bulk of the 1,425 cloths charged at the non-Hanseatic rate of 1s. 9d. per cloth, since the Hansards' privileges were suspended for some of this period (Lloyd, *England and the German Hanse*, pp. 57–9).
- Note 10. The account for Michaelmas 1389 to 15 May 1390 gives its totals of 506½ denizen, 1⅜ alien and 1,018¾ Hanseatic cloths as being for both imports and exports (T.N.A., E356/14, m.13d).
- Note 11. The account for Michaelmas to 8 December 1390 gives its totals of 17 denizen and 208 Hanseatic cloths as being for both imports and exports (T.N.A., E356/14, m. 14).
- Note 12. The alien total for Michaelmas 1465 to 25 March 1467 includes 127 cloths exported by an alien merchant, Alan de Monte Ferrato, on behalf of the king, with customs paid at the alien rate.
- Note 13. The date given in the enrolled account for the start of the account for 1470–71 account overlaps with that for the end of account for 1469–70 (T.N.A., E356/21, m. 30).
- Note 14. Of the 150 cloths exported by aliens in 1472–73, 110 are specified as belonging to merchants of Veere (or 'Caumfer') (see above, pp. 47, 61).
- Note 15. Of the 206 cloths exported by aliens in 1473–74, 193 are specified as belonging to merchants of Veere (see note 14, above).
- Note 16. All 170 cloths exported by aliens in 1474–75 are specified as belonging to merchants of Veere (see note 14 above).
- Note 17. Of the 5 cloths exported by aliens in 1475–76, 1 is specified as belonging to a merchant of Veere (see note 14, above).
- Note 18. All 6 of the cloths exported by aliens in 1476–77 are specified as belonging to the merchants of Veere (see note 14, above).
- Note 19. All 7 of the cloths exported by aliens in 1477–78 are specified as belonging to merchants of Veere (see note 14, above).
- Note 20. All 21 of the cloths exported by aliens in 1478–79 are specified as belonging to merchants of Veere (see note 14, above).
- Note 21. All 8 of the cloths exported by aliens in 1481–82 are specified as belonging to merchants of Veere (see note 14, above).
- Note 22. All of the 55 cloths exported by aliens in 1482–83 are specified as belonging to merchants of Veere (see note 14, above).

Figure 7.2 Cloth exports from Boston, 1353–1548.

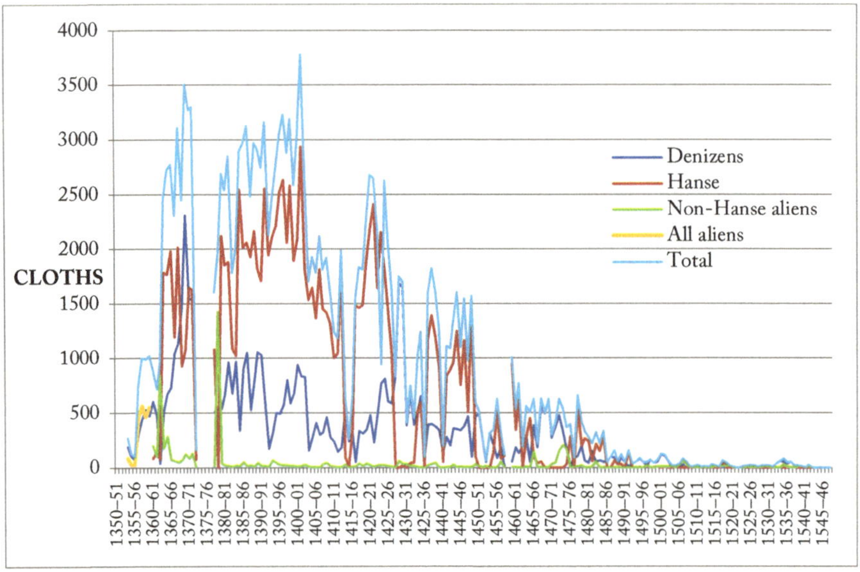

The new cloth customs introduced in 1347 also included a specific duty on exports of worsted, a light, unfulled cloth which was mainly produced in Norfolk and Suffolk and which was made from longer wools than standard 'woollens'.[172] Before this date, denizen exports of worsted were not customed, whilst aliens paid custom on worsted only as part of the *ad valorem* duty of 3d. in the pound, as can be seen in the particular account for February to Michaelmas 1303, when, as noted above, £147 of worsted exports were valued for this custom.[173] The 1347 custom introduced a new duty on denizens of 1d. per single cloth, 2d. per double cloth, 5d. per single 'bed' and 9d. per double 'bed', whilst aliens paid at the higher rate of 1½d. per single cloth, 3d. per double cloth, 7½d. per single bed and 13½d. per double bed.[174] Worsteds could also be charged with the subsidy of poundage (see section 2.9, below).

The situation of Hanseatic merchants in relation to the customs on worsteds is less certain. When the cloth custom was introduced in 1347, a dispute over whether the Hansards were liable to it seems to have arisen at Yarmouth, where the export

172 Amor, *From Wool to Cloth*, pp. 42, 118, 131–2, 141, 161–2, 216; Oldland, *English Woollen Industry*, pp. 1, 21.

173 T.N.A., E122/5/7.

174 Gras, *Early English Customs System*, p. 72; Jenks, *Enrolled Customs Accounts*, Part 3, pp. v–vi; Rigby, *Overseas Trade of Boston*, p. 28; Carus-Wilson and Coleman, *England's Export Trade*, p. 199–200.

trade in worsteds was particularly important. As a result, in 1348, the king's butler, who was at the time responsible for the collection of cloth custom nationally, was instructed that the Hansards should only pay the 1303 *ad valorem* duty on their worsted exports in the port rather than the specific customs introduced on worsteds in 1347.[175] As we have seen above, by the late 1350s disagreement had arisen once more over which customs the Hansards should pay. As part of the resolution of this conflict, the customs collectors in Boston, as in other ports, were told in February 1361 that the Hansards should only pay the 1303 custom for their cloth exports. This meant they were to pay the 1303 *ad valorem* duty on their worsteds rather than the specific customs on worsted which had been introduced in 1347.[176] Certainly, as a particular account for 1365–66 shows, the Hansards were being charged with the *ad valorem* duty on their worsted exports by the Boston customs collectors during this period.[177]

However, the situation changed in 1389. As both the enrolled and particular customs accounts confirm, Hanseatic merchants were regularly charged with the 1347 custom on worsteds at Boston between Michaelmas 1389 and 12 April 1413.[178] As is shown by the Boston particular accounts for 1390–91 and 1397–8, this meant that Hanseatic worsted exports were no longer charged with the custom of 3d. in the pound.[179] A further problem is that since the Hansards were charged with the 1347 duty on worsteds at the same rate as other aliens, their exports may sometimes also have been included in the enrolled accounts amongst the exports of worsteds by 'alien' merchants during this period. For instance, in the two accounts covering the year from Michaelmas 1391, 108 single worsted cloths are given as having been imported and exported by Hansards at Boston (but none by denizens or aliens) before 8 December 1391, whilst the account for the rest of the year notes the export of 443½ single worsted cloths by 'aliens' (but none by denizens or Hansards).[180]

---

175 *Calendar of Patent Rolls, 1348–50*, p. 6.

176 *Calendar of Close Rolls, 1360–64*, p. 152; Lloyd, *England and the German Hanse*, pp. 32–4, 75; Beardwood, *Alien Merchants in England*, pp. 46–8.

177 T.N.A., E122/7/10.

178 For 1389–1413, see Figure 7.3. For the particular accounts, see T.N.A., E122/7/22, mm. 5, 6, 6d; E122/7/23, mm. 4–6d; E122/7/26, m. 1d.; E122/7/31, mm. 3, 3d.; E122/8/2; E122/8/7; Rigby, *Overseas Trade of Boston*, pp. 127, 130, 153, 155–7, 159, 162, 175, 209–10, 22. The Lynn accounts for this period normally refer to 'denizen' and 'alien' exports of worsted, although that for 1398 does specify worsteds exported by Hansards (Jenks, *Enrolled Customs Accounts*, Part 5, pp. 1243–7). The Yarmouth petty custom was farmed for some of this period, but when accounts for it were enrolled, they do not distinguish worsted exports by Hansards (*ibid.*, pp. 1259–69); neither are such exports distinguished in the London accounts for this period (*ibid*, pp. 1215–20).

179 T.N.A., E122/7/22, mm. 5d., 6. 6d..; E122/7/26, m 1d.; E122/7/31, m. 3; Rigby, *Overseas Trade of Boston*, pp. 130–2, 134, 175, 209–10.

180 T.N.A., E356/14, m. 14–14d.

Whether the Hansards were liable to the 1347 duty after 1413 or whether they were once more only charged with the 1303 duty of 3d. in the pound is not clear, although the Boston enrolled accounts do distinguish Hanse worsted exports paying custom at the 1347 rate in 1419–20 and 1437–38.[181]

From 1347 to 1353, the royal butler accounted for the 1347 cloth custom at the Exchequer for all England's ports together and so there are no separate returns for Boston's worsted exports for these years.[182] Figure 7.3 gives the total of worsted exports at Boston from 1353 onwards, with the exception of the period between December 1372 and August 1377, when the custom was farmed (as mentioned above). The totals of all types of worsteds exported in each year in Figure 7.3 are calculated by counting single worsted cloths as one unit, double cloths as two units, single beds as five units and double beds as nine units, in line with the relative rates of customs charged on these cloths.[183] From a low level in the 1350s, worsted exports paying customs in Boston rose rapidly after 1363, reaching over 450 units a year from 1363 to 1372. However, as we have seen, this was a period when the Boston customs jurisdiction was merged with that of Lynn. It is likely that the bulk of the worsted paying custom in Boston at this time was actually shipped from Lynn, rather than from Boston itself, since Lynn, along with Yarmouth, was one of the major ports for the export of East Anglian worsted.[184] Certainly, in the nine years from 1377, when separate figures for Boston are once again available, an annual average of fewer than 30 worsteds was reported as being exported from the port.

For most of the fifteenth and early sixteenth centuries, Boston's recorded worsted exports were at an even lower level than the early 1380s, with entire decades when no custom for worsted was paid in the port at all, with exports nationally declining in the late fourteenth- and early fifteenth centuries.[185] The one exception was the period after 1389, when, as we have seen, Hanseatic merchants suddenly became liable to the 1347 duties on worsted. Thus, whereas an average of only 8 units a year were reported as being exported from Boston in the years 1384–9, almost 500 units a year were customed in the following five years. Exports of worsteds from Boston from 1389 until 1413 were almost entirely dominated by the Hansards, who were, for instance, responsible for all 702 units exported from the port in the year from 2 October 1401, when the worsted trade reached its peak. Nevertheless, the value of worsted exports was relatively minor compared to that of other cloth exports: the value of the worsted exported in 1401–2 was less than 7% of that of the other woollens shipped in that year, even if we use a maximum figure for the price of

181 T.N.A., E356/17, m. 9d; E356/19, m. 36.

182 Jenks, *Enrolled Customs Accounts*, Part 3, pp. 625–7.

183 Carus-Wilson and Coleman, *England's Export Trade*, p. 199, note 5.

184 See Jenks, *Enrolled Customs Accounts*, Part 5, pp. 1244–7, 1262–3.

185 Oldland, *English Woollen Industry*, pp. 42, 114, 153, 208–9; Childs, 'The English export trade in cloth', p. 138.

worsteds.[186] Given the small scale of worsted exports at Boston for most of this period and the distorting effects of the Lynn figures from 1353 to 1372 and of the Hanseatic exports from 1389, the port's worsted exports are not given in graph form below.

Figure 7.3 Worsted exports from Boston, 1353–1548.

	Denizen single cloth	Denizen double cloth	Denizen single bed	Denizen double bed	Alien single cloth	Alien double cloth	Alien single bed	Alien double bed	Hanse single cloth	Hanse double cloth	Hanse double cloth	Hanse single bed	Hanse double bed	Total
20.4.1347–30.7.1353	No returns													
30.7.1353–Mich.1354	0	0	0	0	0	0	0	0	0	0	0	0	0	0
Mich.1354–Mich.1355	0	0	0	0	111.5	0	0	0	0	0	0	0	0	111.5
Mich.1355–Mich.1356	100	0	0	0	0	0	0	0	0	0	0	0	0	100
Mich.1356–30.9.1357	9	0	0	0	70	0	0	0	0	0	0	0	0	79
30.9.1357–Mich.1358	0	0	3	0	0	0	0	0	0	0	0	0	0	15
Mich.1358–Mich.1359	6	0	0	0	58	0	0	0	0	0	0	0	0	64
Mich.1359–Mich.1360	0	0	0	0	12	0	0	0	0	0	0	0	0	12
Mich.1360–Mich.1361	3	0	0	0	0	0	0	0	0	0	0	0	0	15
Mich.1361–Mich.1362	56	0	4	0	0	0	0	0	0	0	0	0	0	76
Mich.1362–18.2.1363	No returns													
18.2.1363–Mich.1363	0	0	5.67	0	6	0	0	0	0	0	0	0	0	34.67
Mich.1363–2.10.1364	410	0	1	0	9	0	0	0	0	0	0	0	0	424
2.10.1364–20.10.1365	738	0	0	0	232	0	11	0	0	0	0	0	0	1095
2.10.1365–Mich.1366	553	0	4	3	160	0	0	0	0	0	0	0	0	760
Mich.1366–Mich.1367	291	0	2	0	48	0	0	0	0	0	0	0	0	244
Mich.1367–Mich.1368	0	0	1	0	0	0	18	0	0	0	0	0	0	278
Mich.1368–Mich.1369	0	0	10	0	0	0	0	0	0	0	0	0	0	50
Mich.1369–Mich.1370	2	0	6	0	0	0	1	0	0	0	0	0	0	19
Mich.1370–Mich.1371	320	0	14	0	0	0	3	0	0	0	0	0	0	405
Mich.1371–Mich.1372	872.5	0	1	0	2	0	1	0	0	0	0	0	0	884.5
Mich.1372–24.12.1372	45	0	0	0	0	0	0	0	0	0	0	0	0	45
24.12.1372–26.8.1377	No returns													

186 Calculated by valuing single worsteds at 15s. each and cloths of assize at £2 each. For these prices, see Gray, 'English foreign trade from 1446 to 1482', pp. 8–9, 361 n.7.

	Denizen single cloth	Denizen double cloth	Denizen single bed	Denizen double bed	Alien single cloth	Alien double cloth	Alien single bed	Alien double bed	Hanse single cloth	Hanse double cloth	Hanse double cloth	Hanse single bed	Hanse double bed	Total	
26.8.1377–Mich.1378	40	0	0	0	124	0	0	0	0	0	0	0	0	164	
Mich.1378–Mich.1379	0	0	0	0	0	0	0	0	0	0	0	0	0	0	Note 1
Mich.1379–Mich.1380	0	0	0	0	0	0	0	0	0	0	0	0	0	0	
Mich.1380–Mich.1381	34	0	0	0	0	0	0	0	0	0	0	0	0	34	
Mich.1381–Mich.1382	28	0	0	0	0	0	0	0	0	0	0	0	0	28	
Mich.1382–Mich.1383	15	0	0	0	0	0	0	0	0	0	0	0	0	15	
Mich.1383–Mich.1384	7	0	0	0	0	0	0	0	0	0	0	0	0	7	Note 2
Mich.1384–Mich.1385	0	0	0	0	0	0	0	0	0	0	0	0	0	0	
Mich.1385–Mich.1386	0	0	0	0	0	0	0	0	0	0	0	0	0	0	
Mich.1386–26.11.1387	0	0	0	0	0	0	0	0	0	0	0	0	0	0	
26.11.1387–Mich.1388	20	0	0	0	0	0	0	0	0	0	0	0	0	20	
Mich.1388–Mich.1389	22	0	0	0	0	0	0	0	0	0	0	0	0	22	
Mich.1389–Mich.1390	21	0	0	0	0	0	0	0	506	0	0	0	0	527	Note 3
Mich.1390–Mich.1391	1	0	0	0	0	0	0	0	451	0	0	0	0	452	
Mich.1391–Mich.1392	0	0	0	0	443.5	0	0	0	108	0	0	0	0	551.5	Note 4
Mich.1392–Mich.1393	0	0	0	0	0	0	0	0	472	0	0	0	0	472	Note 5
Mich.1393–Mich.1394	3	0	0	0	0	0	0	0	448	0	0	0	0	451	
Mich.1394–Mich.1395	16	0	0	0	0	0	0	0	662	0	0	0	0	682	
Mich.1395–Mich.1396	1	0	0	0	0	0	0	0	644	0	0	0	0	645	
Mich.1396–Mich.1397	10	0	0	0	689	0	0	0	0	0	0	0	0	699	
Mich.1397–Mich.1398	27	0	0	0	0	0	0	0	538	0	0	0	0	565	
Mich.1398–Mich.1399	13	0	0	0	674	0	0	0	0	0	0	0	0	687	
Mich.1399–Mich.1400	13	0	0	0	457	1	0	0	0	0	0	0	0	472	
Mich.1400–2.10.1401	0	0	0	0	0	0	0	0	422	0	0	0	0	422	
2.10.1401–2.10.1402	0	0	0	0	0	0	0	0	702	0	0	0	0	702	
2.10.1402–Mich.1403	20	0	0	0	0	0	0	0	563	0	0	0	0	583	
Mich.1403–Mich.1404	0	0	0	0	0	0	0	0	620	0	0	0	0	620	
Mich.1404–Mich.1405	2	0	0	0	0	0	0	0	607	0	0	0	0	609	
Mich.1405–8.9.1406	17	0	0	0	0	0	0	0	658	0	0	0	0	675	Note 6
8.9.1406–Mich.1407	0	0	0	0	0	0	0	0	608	0	0	0	0	608	
Mich.1407–Mich.1408	0	0	0	0	0	0	0	0	451	0	0	0	0	451	
Mich.1408–Mich.1409	0	0	0	0	217	0	0	0	261	0	0	0	0	478	Note 7
Mich.1409–Mich.1410	0	0	0	0	0	0	0	0	361.5	0	0	0	0	371.5	
Mich.1410–Mich.1411	6	0	0	0	387	10	0	0	0	0	0	0	0	413	

	Denizen single cloth	Denizen double cloth	Denizen single bed	Denizen double bed	Alien single cloth	Alien double cloth	Alien single bed	Alien double bed	Hanse single cloth	Hanse double cloth	Hanse double cloth	Hanse single bed	Hanse double bed	Total	
Mich.1411–Mich.1412	0	0	0	0	0	0	0	0	361	0	0	0	0	361	
Mich.1412–Mich.1413	0	0	0	0	383	9	0	0	117	0	0	0	0	518	Note 8
Mich.1413–Mich.1414	32	0	0	0	0	0	0	0	0	0	0	0	0	32	
Mich.1414–Mich.1415	0	0	0	0	0	0	0	0	0	0	0	0	0	0	
Mich.1415–Mich.1416	0	0	0	0	141	1	0	0	0	0	0	0	0	143	
Mich.1416–Mich.1417	0	0	0	0	3	6	0	0	0	0	0	0	0	15	
Mich.1417–Mich.1418	0	0	0	0	1.5	0	0	0	0	0	0	0	0	1.5	
Mich.1418–Mich.1419	0	0	0	0	0	0	0	0	0	0	0	0	0	0	
Mich.1419–10.10.1420	0	0	0	0	0	0	0	0	0	0	0	0	0	8	
10.10.1420–Mich.1421	0	0	0	0	0	0	0	0	0	0	0	0	0	0	
Mich.1421–31.8.1422	0	0	0	0	2	8	0	0	0	0	0	0	0	18	
1.9.1422–Mich.1423	0	0	0	0	3	0	0	0	0	0	0	0	0	3	
Mich.1423–Mich.1424	4	0	2	0	0	0	0	0	0	0	0	0	0	14	
Mich.1424–Mich.1425	0	3	0	0	0	4.5	0	0	0	0	0	0	0	15	
Mich.1425–Mich.1426	0	5	0	0	0	4	0	0	0	0	0	0	0	18	
Mich.1426–Mich.1427	0	0	0	0	0	0	0	0	0	0	0	0	0	0	
Mich.1427–Mich.1428	0	1	0	0	0	0	0	0	0	0	0	0	0	2	
Mich.1428–1.11.1429	0	0	0	0	0	1	0	0	0	0	0	0	0	2	
1.11.1429–1.11.1430	0	0	0	0	0	0	0	0	0	0	0	0	0	0	
1.11.1430–20.10.1431	0	0	0	0	0	0	0	0	0	0	0	0	0	0	
20.10.1431–Mich.1432	0	0	0	0	0	2.5	0	0	0	0	0	0	0	5	
Mich.1432–Mich.1433	0	0	0	0	0	0	0	0	0	0	0	0	0	0	
Mich.1433–Mich.1434	0	3	0	0	0	0	0	0	0	0	0	0	0	6	
Mich.1434–Mich.1435	0	0	0	0	0	0	0	0	0	0	0	0	0	0	
Mich.1435–10.10.1436	0	0	0	0	0	0	0	0	0	0	0	0	0	0	
10.10.1436–11.11.1437	0	0	0	0	1.5	6.5	0	0	0	0	0	0	0	14.5	
11.11.1437–Mich.1438	0	0	0	0	0	0	0	0	0	0	0	0	0	6	
Mich.1438–Mich.1439	0	0	0	0	0	0	0	0	0	0	0	0	0	0	
Mich.1439–Mich.1440	0	6	0	0	0	0	0	0	0	0	0	0	0	12	
Mich.1440–31.6.1441	0	0	0	0	0	0	0	0	0	0	0	0	0	0	
31.6.1441–Mich.1442	0	0	0	0	0	0	0	0	0	0	0	0	0	0	
Mich.1442–12.8.1443	0	0	0	0	0	0	0	0	0	0	0	0	0	0	
12.8.1443–12.10.1444	0	0	0	0	0	4	0	0	0	0	0	0	0	8	
12.10.1444–12.10.1445	0	0	0	0	0	10	0	0	0	0	0	0	0	20	

	Denizen single cloth	Denizen double cloth	Denizen single bed	Denizen double bed	Alien single cloth	Alien double cloth	Alien single bed	Alien double bed	Hanse single cloth	Hanse double cloth	Hanse double cloth	Hanse single bed	Hanse double bed	Total
12.10.1445–24.6.1446	0	0	0	0	0	2	0	0	0	0	0	0	0	4
24.6.1446–18.7.1447	0	1	0	0	0	6	0	0	0	0	0	0	0	14
18.7.1447–21.11.1448	0	0	0	0	0	1	0	0	0	0	0	0	0	2
21.11.1448–Mich.1458	0	0	0	0	0	0	0	0	0	0	0	0	0	0
Mich.1458–15.12.1459	No returns													
15.12.1459–2.5.1465	0	0	0	0	0	0	0	0	0	0	0	0	0	0
2.5.1465–Mich.1465	0	0	0	0	0	3	0	0	0	0	0	0	0	6
Mich.1465–25.3.1467	0	0	0	0	0	0	0	0	0	0	0	0	0	0
25.3.1467–6.3.1468	0	0	0	0	0	0	0	0	0	0	0	0	0	0
6.3.1468–25.12.1468	21	0	0	0	0	0	0	0	0	0	0	0	0	21
25.12.1468–Mich.1507	0	0	0	0	0	0	0	0	0	0	0	0	0	0
Mich.1507–Mich.1508	0	0	0	0	0	16	0	0	0	0	0	0	0	32
Mich.1508–Mich.1511	0	0	0	0	0	0	0	0	0	0	0	0	0	0
Mich.1511–Mich.1512	0	2	0	0	0	0	0	0	0	0	0	0	0	4
Mich.1512–Mich.1517	0	0	0	0	0	0	0	0	0	0	0	0	0	0
Mich.1517–Mich.1518	0	0	0	0	0	2	0	0	0	0	0	0	0	4
Mich.1518–Mich.1519	0	0	0	0	0	7	0	0	0	0	0	0	0	14
Mich.1519–Mich.1520	0	0	0	0	0	6	0	0	0	0	0	0	0	12
Mich.1520–Mich.1521	0	0	0	0	0	5.5	0	0	0	0	0	0	0	11
Mich.1521–Mich.1522	0	0	0	0	0	0	0	0	0	0	0	0	0	0
Mich.1522–Mich.1523	0	0	0	0	0	5	0	0	0	0	0	0	0	10
Mich.1523–Mich.1524	0	0	0	0	0	0	0	0	0	0	0	0	0	0
Mich.1524–Mich.1525	0	0	0	0	0	0	0	0	0	0	0	0	0	0
Mich.1525–Mich.1526	0	0	0	0	0	0	0	0	0	0	0	0	0	6
Mich.1526–Mich.1527	0	0	0	0	0	0	0	0	0	0	0	0	0	0
Mich.1527–Mich.1528	0	0	0	0	0	0	0	0	0	0	0	0	0	0
Mich.1528–Mich.1529	0	0	0	0	0	7	0	0	0	0	0	0	0	14
Mich.1529–Mich.1530	0	0	0	0	0	4.5	0	0	0	0	0	0	0	9
Mich.1530–Mich.1538	0	0	0	0	0	0	0	0	0	0	0	0	0	0
Mich.1538–Mich.1539	0	0	0	0	0	5.5	0	0	0	0	0	0	0	11
Mich.1539–Mich.1540	0	0	0	0	0	7.5	0	0	0	0	0	0	0	14
Mich.1540–Mich.1541	0	0	0	0	0	3	0	0	0	0	0	0	0	6
Mich.1541–Mich.1542	0	0	0	0	0	0	0	0	0	0	0	0	0	0

	Denizen single cloth	Denizen double cloth	Denizen single bed	Denizen double bed	Alien single cloth	Alien double cloth	Alien single bed	Alien double bed	Hanse single cloth	Hanse double cloth	Hanse double cloth	Hanse single bed	Hanse double bed	Total
Mich.1542–Mich.1543	0	0	0	0	0	1.5	0	0	0	0	0	0	0	3
Mich.1543–Mich.1544	0	0	0	0	0	0	0	0	0	0	0	0	0	0
Mich.1544–Mich.1545	0	0	0	0	0	2	0	0	0	0	0	0	0	4
Mich.1545–Mich.1548	0	0	0	0	0	0	0	0	0	0	0	0	0	0

(Source: T.N.A., E356 enrolled customs accounts)

Notes to Figure 7.3:

- Note 1. The account for 1378–79 includes 18 single worsted cloths said to have been imported by denizens (T.N.A., E356/14, m. 11d).
- Note 2. The 7 single worsted cloths on which denizen merchants paid custom in 1383–84 are said to have been 'imported and exported' (T.N.A., E356/14, m. 12).
- Note 3. The account for Michaelmas 1389 to 15 May 1390 includes 15 single denizen worsteds and 268 belonging to Hansards which are said to have been 'imported or exported' (T.N.A., E356/14, m. 13d).
- Note 4. The two accounts covering the year from Michaelmas 1391 include 108 single worsted cloths imported and exported by Hansards before 8 December 1391, and 443½ single worsted cloths exported by aliens after 8 December (T.N.A., E356/14, m. 14–14d). Since Hansards and aliens paid the custom at the same rate, it is not possible to know whether the worsted exported in the second part of the year actually belonged to Hansards
- Note 5. The account for 1392–93 says that 472 single beds of worsted were exported by Hansards (T.N.A., E356/14, m. 14d). However, since these exports paid at the rate for single cloths, it is likely that this is a scribal error. They have thus been included in the total for single cloths here.
- Note 6. The account for 1405–6 includes 642 Hanse single worsted cloths charged at the standard rate of 1½d. per cloth, but it also includes 12 cloths paying at 2d. per cloth, which have been included in the Hanse total here at the rate of 1.33 cloths each (T.N.A., E356/17, m. 6).
- Note 7. The three accounts covering the year from Michaelmas 1408 include 217 single worsted cloths exported by alien merchants before 28 January 1409 and 261 single worsted exported by Hansards after 8 May 1409 (T.N.A., E356/177–7d). Since Hansards and aliens paid custom at the same rate, it is not possible to know how much of the worsted exported by aliens before 28 January actually belonged to Hansards.

- Note 8. The three accounts covering the year from Michaelmas 1412 include 117 single worsted cloths specified as having been exported by Hansards before 12 April 1413, and 383 single worsted and 9 double worsteds as exported by aliens after 12 April (T.N.A., E356/17, m. 8–8d). Since Hansards and aliens paid the custom at the same rate, it is not possible to know how much of the worsted exported by aliens after 12 April actually belonged to Hansards.

2.8 Alien and denizen wine imports, 1322–1548

In addition to the duties imposed in 1303 on wool, hides, cloth, wax and miscellaneous goods, the new custom introduced a levy on wine imports by alien merchants at the rate of 2s. per tun of wine (a tun was the equivalent of 2 pipes, 4 hogsheads or 252 gallons). Since this custom was a commutation of the ancient royal right of prise, by which the king had the right to one or two tuns from each ship arriving with wine in England, it was administered separately from the rest of the new custom, being the responsibility of the king's chief butler, who appointed his own deputies in each head port. In practice, these deputies in Boston were often the same men who were commissioned to collect the other royal customs and subsidies in the port. Nevertheless, they usually accounted for the duty on wine separately rather than in the particular and enrolled accounts of other duties.[187] An exception was the brief period from 1322 to 1325, when the returns for the custom of 2s. per tun paid by alien merchants were included alongside the enrolled accounts of the other customs. The figures for alien wine imports for these years are given in Figure 8.1[188] The study of the wine trade by James, which drew on the accounts of the chief butler as well as the enrolled customs accounts, provides the totals for alien imports of wine at Boston for various years between 1322 to 1395. For the sake of completeness, these totals are provided in Figure 8.2[189]

For a more comprehensive record of wine imports at Boston we must turn to the subsidy of tunnage. This subsidy, which was paid by both denizen and alien merchants, was first introduced in 1340 and was usually granted by parliament alongside the *ad valorem* duty of poundage (see section 2.9, below).[190] In the fourteenth century, tunnage and poundage were sometimes collected at Boston by the

187 James, *Studies in the Medieval Wine Trade*, p. 4; Rigby, *Overseas Trade of Boston*, pp. xix–xx. Boston is omitted from the list of ports where butlerage was collected in R. Blackmore, *Government and Merchant Finance in the Anglo-Gascon Trade, 1300–1500* (London, 2020), p. 225.

188 T.N.A., E356/2, m. 33; Jenks, *Enrolled Customs Accounts*, Part 3, pp. 216–7.

189 James, *Studies in the Medieval Wine Trade*, Appendices 14, 15. See also Beardwood, *Alien Merchants in England*, pp. 178–80.

190 W. M. Ormrod, 'The origins of tunnage and poundage: parliament and the estate of merchants in the fourteenth century', *Parliamentary History*, 28 (2009), pp. 209–27.

officials responsible for the port's other customs, as they were in the 1380s, but at other times, as in the 1390s, separate collectors were appointed to collect tunnage and poundage in the port. In either case, however, tunnage and poundage were accounted for separately from the great and petty customs.[191] By contrast, from 1432 onwards, one pair of collectors accounted for all of the customs and subsidies levied in the port, apart from the 2s. per tun levied by the butler's deputy, and they did so in a single composite account.

In the earliest surviving tunnage account, for 1350, the subsidy was levied at the rate of 1s. per tun of wine, whilst that for 1350–1 was charged at 3s. 4d. per tun. In 1383–4 and 1386–7, the rate was 2s. per tun, but from 1388 it was levied at a standard rate of 3s. per tun of non-sweet wine imported by denizens or aliens, with the exception of 1401–03 when it was again 2s. Prior to 1437, Hanseatic merchants were liable to tunnage and poundage, but after this date they were exempt apart from short periods in 1447–49 and 1454–55 (see section 2.9, below). Since, however, the Hansards played little part in Boston's wine trade, these changes do not really affect the impression of trade given in the customs accounts (see Figures 8.3 and 8.4). More significant for the interpretation of the tunnage returns are the exemptions from tunnage enjoyed by denizen merchants from 1 September 1422 to 1 August 1425, 12 November 1427 to 4 April 1428, 4 April 1429 to 6 December 1429, and 11 November 1436 to 1 April 1437.[192]

A further distinction drawn in the enrolled accounts is that for imports of sweet wine by alien merchants, who, from 1431, were charged with an extra 3s. per tun of wine over and above the 3s. per tun which was charged on all wine imports.[193] This sweet wine, which was made from sun-dried, raisin-like grapes, originated in the eastern Mediterranean. It was sometimes specified in the enrolled accounts as being either malmsey (which was mainly shipped from Monemvasia in the eastern Peloponnese) or Romeney wine (which came from the southern Peoloponnese and was mainly exported via Methoni).[194] Non-sweet wine was usually referred to simply as 'wine' in the enrolled accounts, but was occasionally specified as being red, white, Gascon, Rhenish or La Rochelle wine.[195] In practice, although some wine from Anjou and the Rhineland was brought to Boston, Gascony was the main source of the wine imported there.[196]

---

191 In the 1380s, separate controllers were sometimes appointed for tunnage and poundage and for Boston's other customs, but from 1391 a single controller oversaw the collection of all of the port's duties (Rigby, *Overseas Trade of Boston*, pp. xix, 222).

192 Jenks, *Enrolled Customs Accounts*, Part 6, p. iv.

193 Gras, *Early English Customs System*, pp. 83–4; *Calendar of Fine Rolls, 1461–71*, p. 6; Jenks, *Enrolled Customs Accounts*, Part 6, p. iv.

194 S. Rose, *The Wine Trade in Medieval Europe, 1000–1500* (London, 2011), pp. 15, 101–2. For malmsey and Romeney wine, see, for instance, T.N.A., E356/26, m. 20; E356/27, mm. 5d.,6.

195 See, for instance, T.N.A., E356/19, m. 37d; E356/20, mm. 25, 29.

196 Rigby, 'Medieval Boston', p. 11.

In a number of Boston enrolled accounts between 1388 and 1422, tunnage is said to have been paid on wine which had been 'imported or exported' ('*adducta quam educta*'), a formulation also used in the accounts of other ports.[197] Since some of the London enrolled accounts do distinguish wine imports paying tunnage from exports which were charged with the subsidy, it is, in theory, possible that some of the wine paying tunnage at Boston had also been exported (or re-exported).[198] It is likely, however, that the vast bulk of this wine had actually been imported. Certainly, all of the wine listed in the port's surviving particular accounts for Richard II's reign was imported.[199] This was also the case for the 101½ tuns paying tunnage between Michaelmas and 8 December 1391, which the enrolled account claims to have been '*traducta*' that the particular account shows as having been imported.[200]

The tunnage accounts provide us with the totals of wine shipped by both non-Hanseatic aliens and by denizen merchants. Figures 8.3 and 8.4 give the total amount, in tuns, of sweet and non-sweet wine imported at Boston from the mid-fourteenth century onwards, although a regular series of accounts only survives from the 1380s. Since alien and denizen imports of non-sweet wine paid tunnage at the same rate, there was, in theory, no reason for them to be distinguished in the enrolled accounts. In practice, however, accounts for some years, especially from the late fifteenth century onwards, do distinguish denizen imports from those by aliens. For such cases, Figure 8.3 gives separate totals for each of them. Figure 8.3 also distinguishes alien and denizen imports in the years 1350 to 1351 and 1392 to 1395 using the information for alien imports given by James (see Figure 8.2). Figures 8.3 and 8.4 include the totals of both sweet and non-sweet wine imports at Boston, since, as can be seen from Figure 8.5, which lists all mentions of sweet wine in Boston's enrolled customs accounts after 12 January 1431, the trade in sweet wine in Boston (as in England as a whole) was of much less significance than that in Gascon non-sweet wine.[201] As Figure 8.5 shows, the accounts sometimes distinguish the imports of sweet wine by denizen merchants even though they were not actually liable to the additional 3s. per tun subsidy which was paid by aliens on their sweet wine imports.[202] The equalization of customs rates between denizens and aliens for seven years from April in 1539 (see section 2.6, above) meant that aliens were exempt from the extra 3s. per tun charged on their imports of sweet

197 T.N.A., E356/5, mm. 26d.-32; E356/15, mm. 1d., 10, 21, 23. See also the 8 tuns said to have been exported by denizens at Boston in 1428 (T.N.A., E356/16, m. 11). For other ports, see Jenks, *Enrolled Customs Accounts*, Part 2, pp. 512–15.

198 Jenks, *Enrolled Customs Accounts*, Part 6, pp. 1405, 1446.

199 T.N.A., E122/7/17; E122/7/19; E122/7/20; E122/7/21; E122/7/22; E122/7/23; E122/7/27; E122/7/30. See the index entry for 'wine' in Rigby, *Overseas Trade of Boston*, p. 281.

200 T.N.A., E356/5, m. 28; T.N.A., E122/7/24.

201 James, *Studies in the Medieval Wine Trade*, p. xv.

202 Denizen sweet wine was charged at 6s. per tun in 1434–35 (T.N.A., E356/18, m.10).

wine. Nevertheless, the enrolled accounts for this period continued to distinguish these imports from those of non-sweet wines, even though the same rates of subsidy were now being paid on both types of wine.[203]

The accounts of the royal butler and the enrolled tunnage accounts reveal the radical changes which occurred over the course of the fourteenth century in the volume of Boston's wine imports and in the merchants responsible for shipping them. The figures for the royal wine prise for 1300–01 give a total of 1,713 tuns imported by denizens and aliens at Boston, meaning that the port ranked second only to London in the trade at this time.[204] Imports by aliens, primarily Gascons, who dominated the trade at Boston at this time, remained buoyant in the 1320s and early 1330s, averaging over 1,000 tuns a year, but then fell to around a half of this level in the mid-1330s before plummeting with the outbreak of the Hundred Years' War in 1337. The Anglo–French truce of the early 1340s allowed a partial revival of alien imports to around 300 tuns a year, but the renewal of the war in 1345 and then the disruption caused by the Black Death were disastrous for the trade and no alien imports were recorded at Boston between 1348 and 1353. Even after partially recovering in the mid-1350s, alien imports were still only around 200 tuns a year, falling to around 100 tuns in the 1360s, with a further decline to around 30 tuns a year by the mid-1390s. In Boston, as in other English ports, denizens came to control the Gascon wine trade, with English merchants accounting for about 90 % of around 300 tuns a year entering the port in the mid-1390s. However, the rise of denizen merchants in the trade meant that wine was increasingly shipped to London and the ports of the south-west, where denizens had always controlled a larger share of wine imports than they had in the ports of the east coast. Thus, from 1418, imports of wine at Boston declined further, even though imports nationally were, at first, stable. Similarly, in the mid-fifteenth century, whilst England's wine imports slumped during the final stages of the Hundred Years' War and the continued Anglo–French hostilities afterwards, at Boston they almost totally disappeared. Nationally, the wine trade recovered after 1485, with imports now exceeding the levels of a century earlier, although they did not regain the levels of the early fourteenth century. Now, however, most wine was imported via London and Bristol, with Boston's decline being even more marked than that of other east coast ports. Thus, even in the late 1530s and early 1540s, when the trade at Boston enjoyed a slight revival, a total of only around 120 tuns of wine a year was brought in there, mainly by denizens, a far cry from the 1,000 tuns or more a year which aliens alone had imported in the 1320s.[205]

---

203 T.N.A., E356/27, mm. 5d-6.

204 James, *Studies in the Medieval Wine Trade*, Appendix 10.

205 James, *Studies in the Medieval Wine Trade*, 39, 42, 45–50, 93–4; Rigby, 'Boston and Grimsby in the Middle Ages', pp. 206–8, 216, 222, 368–9; Kowaleski, 'Port towns', pp. 480–1; Rose, *The Wine Trade in Medieval Europe*, p. 69; Blackmore, *Government and Merchant Finance in the Anglo-Gascon Trade*, pp. 21–4, 31–2, 44–5.

Figure 8.1 Alien wine imports at Boston, 1322–1325 (tuns).

20.7.1322–Michaelmas 1323	1,007
10.10.1323–1323-Michaelmas 1324	1,568
Michaelmas 1324–Michaelmas 1325	0

(Source: T.N.A., Enrolled customs account, E356/2, m. 33)

Figure 8.2 Alien wine imports at Boston, 1322–1395 (tuns).

20.7.1322–15.5.1323	757	
15.5.1323–15.5.1324	1568	
Mich.1324–Mich.1325	0	
Mich.1325–Mich.1326	972	
Mich.1326–Mich.1327	No return	
Mich.1327–Mich.1328	1175	
Mich.1328–Mich.1329	1151	
Mich.1328–Mich.1330	No returns	
Mich.1330–Mich.1331	909	
Mich.1331–Mich.1332	1313	
5.5.1333–Mich.1333	80	
Mich.1333–Mich.1334	1474	
Mich.1334–Mich.1335	895	
Mich.1335–Mich.1337	228	Note 1
15.2.1338–Mich.1339	445	
Mich.1339–Mich.1340	0	
Mich.1340–Mich.1341	318	
Mich.1341–Mich.1342	312	
Mich.1342–Mich.1343	405	
Mich.1343–Mich.1344	No return	
Mich.1344–Mich.1345	173	
Mich.1345–Mich.1346	258	
Mich.1346–Mich.1347	0	
Mich.1347–Mich.1348	319	
Mich.1348–Mich.1349	0	
Mich.1349–Mich.1350	0	
Mich.1350–Mich.1351	0	
Mich.1351–Mich.1352	0	
Mich.1352–Mich.1353	0	
Mich.1353–Mich.1354	36	
Mich.1354–Mich.1355	297	
Mich.1355–Mich.1356	400	
Mich.1356–Mich.1357	No return	
Mich.1357–Mich.1358	121	
Mich.1358–Mich.1359	99	
Mich.1359–Mich.1360	218	
Mich.1360–Mich.1361	0	
Mich.1361–Mich.1362	225	
Mich.1363–Mich.1364	98	
Mich.1364–Mich.1365	191	
Mich.1365–Mich.1366	No return	
Mich.1366–Mich.1367	15	
Mich.1367–Mich.1368	36	
Mich.1368–Mich.1370	No returns	
Mich.1370–Mich.1371	4	
Mich.1371–Mich.1372	10	
Mich.1372–Mich.1378	No returns	
Mich.1378–Mich.1379	125	
Mich.1379–Mich.1380	40	
Mich.1380–Mich.1381	45	
Mich.1381–Mich.1382	5	
Mich.1381–Mich.1392	No returns	
Mich.1392–Mich.1393	29	
Mich.1393–Mich.1394	10	
Mich.1394–Mich.1395	46	

(Source: James, Studies in the Medieval Wine Trade, Appendices 14 and 15)

Figure 8.3 Total denizen and alien sweet and non-sweet wine imports at Boston, 1350–1548 (tuns).

	Denizen	Alien	Total	
28.2.1350–28.6.1350	70	0	70	Note 1
29.9.1350–30.9.1351	249.5	0	249.5	Note 2
2.12.1383–Mich.1384			244.5	
24.11.1386–28.11.1387			190	
20.3.1388–29.7.1388	218	0	218	
29.7.1388–24.6.1389			373	
24.6.1389–2.2.1390			100.5	
1.3.1390–30.11.1390			96	
30.11.1390–Mich.1391			123	
Mich.1391–Mich.1392			229	
Mich.1392–Mich.1393	137.5	29	166.5	Note 3
Mich.1393–Mich.1394	440.5	10	450.5	Note 4
Mich.1394–Mich.1395	336.5	46	382.25	Note 5
Mich.1395–Mich.1396			173.05	
Mich.1396–Mich.1397			188.5	
Mich.1397–Mich.1398			230.25	
Mich.1398–15.9.1399			307.125	
3.4.1401–25.6.1402			390.5	
25.6.1402–15.4.1403			265	
15.4.1403–Mich.1403			40	
Mich.1403–Mich.1404			302.5	
Mich.1404–Mich.1405			113	
Mich.1405–Mich.1406			226.5	
Mich.1406–Mich.1407			53.5	
Mich.1407–Mich.1408			224	
Mich.1408–Mich.1409			268.5	
Mich.1409–Mich.1410			327.5	
Mich.1410–Mich.1411			337.5	
Mich.1411–Mich.1412			267.5	
Mich.1412–Mich.1413			354	
Mich.1413–Mich.1414			463	
Mich.1414–Mich.1415			348	
Mich.1415–Mich.1416			246	
Mich.1416–Mich.1417			327.5	
Mich.1417–Mich.1418	318.5	0	318.5	
Mich.1418–Mich.1419			191	

	Denizen	Alien	Total	
Mich.1419–10.10.1420			169.25	
10.10.1420–Mich.1421	100.75	0	100.75	
Mich.1421–31.8.1422	73.25	73.25	73.25	
1.9.1422–Mich.1423	0	35.75	35.75	
Mich.1423–Mich.1424	0	4	4	
Mich.1424–Mich.1425	0	4	4	
Mich.1425–Mich.1426	0	138	138	
Mich.1426–Mich.1427	175.25	1.58	176.83	
Mich.1427–Mich.1428	8	2	10	
Mich.1428–1.11.1429	205.75	2.75	208.5	
1.11.1429–1.11.1430			289	
1.11.1430–20.10.1431	180	0.5	180.5	
20.10.1431–Mich.1432			151.5	
Mich.1432–Mich.1433			39.5	
Mich.1433–Mich.1434			56.5	
Mich.1434–Mich.1435			143	
Mich.1435–10.10.1436	2	0	2	
10.10.1436–11.11.1437			0	
11.11.1437–Mich.1438			12.5	
Mich.1438–Mich.1439			2	
Mich.1439–Mich.1440	1	0	1	
Mich.1440–30.6.1441			7.5	
30.6.1441–Mich.1442			10.5	
Mich.1442–12.8.1443			55	
12.8.1443–12.10.1444			10.5	
12.10.1444–12.10.1445			22	
12.10.1445–24.6.1446			15.5	
24.6.1446–18.7.1447			6.5	
18.7.1447–21.11.1448			6	
21.11.1448–21.11.1449			91.5	
21.11.1449–Mich.1450			7.75	
Mich.1450–3.2.1452	4.5	0	4.5	
3.2.1452–Mich.1452			0	
Mich.1452–Mich.1453			35	
Mich.1453–Mich.1454			6.75	
Mich.1454–10.10.1455			0	
10.10.1455–10.10.1456			2	
10.10.1456–Mich.1457			0	
Mich.1457–Mich.1458	2.5	0	2.5	

	Denizen	Alien	Total	
Mich.1458–15.12.1459			No returns	
15.12.1459–1.9.1460			0	
1.9.1460–Mich.1461			0.75	
Mich.1461–Mich.1462	10.25	10.25	10.25	
Mich.1462–20.7.1463			3	
20.7.1463–25.2.1465			1.5	
25.2.1465–Mich.1465			38.5	
Mich.1465–25.3.1466	7.75	0	7.75	
25.3.1466–25.3.1467			1.5	
25.3.1467–6.3.1468			18	
6.3.1468–25.12.1468			24.25	
25.12.1468–Mich.1469			5.25	
Mich.1469–13.11.1470	7.5	0	7.5	Note 6
26.10.1470–Mich.1471	0.5	0	0.5	Note 7
Mich.1471–8.10.1472			3.5	
8.10.1472–8.10.1473			3.5	
8.10.1473–2.11.1474	0	1.5	1.5	
2.11.1474–Mich.1475	0	2.5	2.5	
Mich.1475–Mich.1476			18.5	
Mich.1476–Mich.1477	16	1	17	Note 8
Mich.1477–Mich.1478			22.5	
Mich.1478–Mich.1479	1.25	0	1.25	
Mich.1479–Mich.1480	5.75	0	5.75	
Mich.1480–Mich.1481	37	0	37	
Mich.1481–Mich.1482	0.5	0	0.5	
Mich.1482–Mich.1483	5	0	5	
Mich.1483–Mich.1484	26.75	2	28.75	
Mich.1484–Mich.1485	15.5	0	15.5	
Mich.1485–Mich.1486	40	0	40	
Mich.1486–Mich.1487	1	0	1	
Mich.1487–Mich.1488	47.75	0	47.75	
Mich.1488–Mich.1489	44	0	44	
Mich.1489–Mich.1490	7.5	0	7.5	
Mich.1490–Mich.1491	79.25	0	79.25	
Mich.1491–Mich.1492	0.5	0	0.5	
Mich.1492–Mich.1493	26.5	0	26.5	
Mich.1493–Mich.1494	24	0	24	
Mich.1494–Mich.1495	78	0	78	
Mich.1495–Mich.1496	101	0	101	

	Denizen	Alien	Total	
Mich.1496–Mich.1497	9.5	8	17.5	
Mich.1497–Mich.1498	73	0	73	
Mich.1498–Mich.1499	40.75	0	40.75	
Mich.1499–Mich.1500	58.75	27.125	85.875	
Mich.1500–Mich.1501	94.25	0	94.25	
Mich.1501–Mich.1502	34	0	34	
Mich.1502–Mich.1503			102	
Mich.1503–Mich.1504	73	0	73	
Mich.1504–Mich.1505			61.75	
Mich.1505–Mich.1506			59	
Mich.1506–Mich.1507			47.25	
Mich.1507–Mich.1508	11.75	0	11.75	
Mich.1508–Mich.1509	11.75	0	11.75	
Mich.1509–Mich.1510	6	3	9	
Mich.1510–Mich.1511	50.5	10.5	62	
Mich.1511–Mich.1512	87	26	113	
Mich.1512–Mich.1513	7	0	7	
Mich.1513–Mich.1514	10.5	0	10.5	
Mich.1514–Mich.1515	39.25	4	43.25	
Mich.1515–Mich.1516	38.5	0	38.5	
Mich.1516–Mich.1517	57	23	80	
Mich.1517–Mich.1518	111.25	3.5	114.75	
Mich.1518–Mich.1519	61.75	13	74.75	
Mich.1519–Mich.1520	144.25	0	144.25	
Mich.1520–Mich.1521	127.25	0.75	128	
Mich.1521–Mich.1522	58.5	0	58.5	
Mich.1522–Mich.1523	6	0	6	
Mich.1523–Mich.1524	0	6	6	
Mich.1524–Mich.1525			0	
Mich.1525–Mich.1526	57	0	57	
Mich.1526–Mich.1527	55	0	55	
Mich.1527–Mich.1528	4	0	4	
Mich.1528–Mich.1529	80.167	0	80.167	
Mich.1529–Mich.1530	65.75	0	65.75	
Mich.1530–Mich.1531	84.25	0.25	84.5	
Mich.1531–Mich.1532	79.25	8	87.25	
Mich.1532–Mich.1533	89.75	0	89.75	
Mich.1533–Mich.1534	137.5	0	137.5	
Mich.1534–Mich.1535	222.5	0	222.5	

	Denizen	Alien	Total	
Mich.1535–Mich.1536	129.75	0	129.75	
Mich.1536–Mich.1537	91.5	0	91.5	
Mich.1537–Mich.1538	164.25	0	164.25	
Mich.1538–Mich.1539	78.5	4	82.5	
Mich.1539–Mich.1540	117.75	0.5	118.25	
Mich.1540–Mich.1541	142.75	0	142.75	
Mich.1541–Mich.1542	125.5	1	126.5	
Mich.1542–Mich.1543	0	0.5	0.5	
Mich.1543–Mich.1544	0	3	3	
Mich.1544–Mich.1545	24	0	24	
Mich.1545–Mich.1546	38	0	38	
Mich.1546–Mich.1547	108	0	108	
Mich.1547–Mich.1548	44.5	16	60.75	

(Source: T.N.A., E356 Enrolled customs accounts)

Notes to Figure 8.3:

- Note 1. The figures for total wine imports for 1350–1 are drawn from the enrolled tunnage accounts; the separate figures for alien and denizen imports are calculated using the separate totals for alien imports given in James, *Studies in the Medieval Wine Trade*, Appendix 15.
- Note 2. See note 1, above.
- Note 3. The figures for total wine imports for 1392–5 are drawn from the enrolled tunnage accounts; the separate figures for alien and denizen imports are calculated using the totals of alien imports given in James, *Studies in the Medieval Wine Trade*, Appendix 15.
- Note 4. See note 3, above.
- Note 5. See note 3, above.
- Note 6. Dates as given in the enrolled account.
- Note 7. Dates as given in the enrolled account.
- Note 8. Including 1 tun imported by a merchant of Veere.

Figure 8.4 Total of denizen and alien sweet and non-sweet wine imports at Boston, 1388–1548 (tuns).

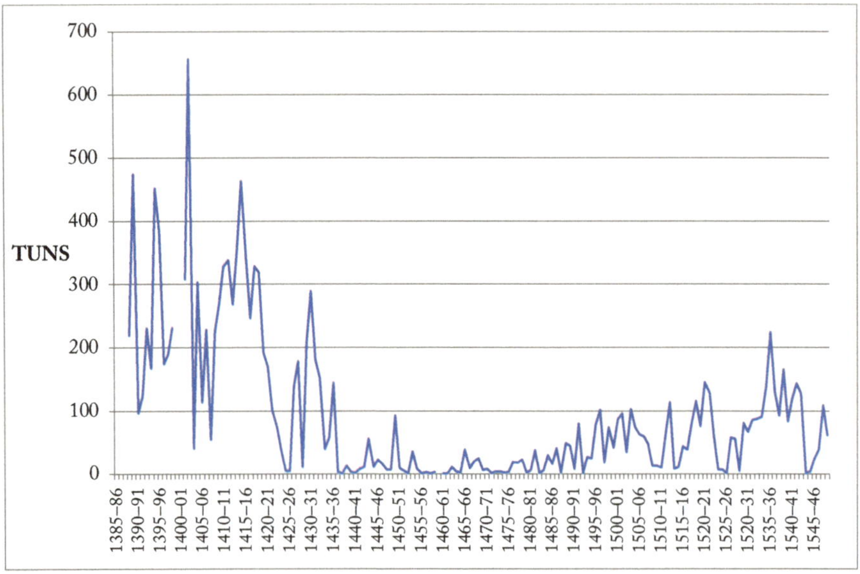

Figure 8.5 Sweet wine imports at Boston, 1431–1548.

12.1.1431–20.10.1431	1 pipe (alien)
Mich.1434–Mich.1435	2 tuns (denizen)
30.9.1436–10.10.1436	2 tuns (denizen)
Mich.1438–Mich.1439	1 tun (alien)
30.6.1441–Mich.1442	2/3 of a tun (alien)
Mich.1442–21 April 1443	1½ tuns (alien)
10.10.1455–10.10.1456	1 tun (alien)
9.10.1499–15.2.1500	1 pipe and ½ hogshead (alien)
Mich.1500–Mich.1501	2 tuns, 1 pipe and 1 hogshead (denizen)
Mich.1502–Mich.1503	1 pipe
Mich. 1507–Mich.1508	2 tuns, 1 pipe (denizen)
Mich.1509–Mich.1510	3 tuns (alien) and 2 tuns (denizen)
Mich.1510–Mich.1511	1 pipe (alien)
Mich.1520–Mich.1521	1 pipe (alien)
Mich.1522–Mich.1523	6 tuns (denizen)
Mich.1523–Mich.1524	6 tuns (alien)
Mich.1532–Mich.1533	5 tuns (denizen)

Mich.1542–Mich.1543	½ tun (alien)
Mich.1543–Mich.1544	3 tuns (alien)

(Source: T.N.A., E356 Enrolled customs accounts)

2.9 Alien and denizen imports and exports liable to poundage, 1347–1548

Parliamentary grants of tunnage were usually also accompanied by a grant of the *ad valorem* duty of poundage. This subsidy was first collected in 1340. The earliest surviving poundage returns date from 1347, but, as with tunnage, returns for this subsidy only survive continuously from the 1380s.[206] As we have seen, the men who were appointed as collectors of tunnage and poundage in Boston were sometimes different from those responsible for the other duties collected there. However, even when the same men were responsible for both tunnage and poundage and the other customs duties levied in the port, separate accounts were initially compiled for the subsidy. It was only from 1432 that a single, composite enrolled account was created for all the customs and subsidies levied in Boston. Prior to Michaelmas 1384, poundage was paid at the rate of 6d. in the pound.[207] After this date, it was normally levied at the rate of 12d. in the pound, exceptions being from 1 March to 30 November 1390, when it was again 6d. in the pound; 3 April 1401 to 15 April 1403, when it was charged at 8d. in the pound; and from Michaelmas 1432 to Easter 1433 when non-Hanseatic aliens paid 18d. in the pound, whereas denizen and Hanseatic merchants paid at the standard rate of 12d. in the pound.[208]

In 1454, the rate of poundage on exports of tin and of pewter vessels by non-Hanseatic aliens was raised from the standard 1s. to 2s. in the pound.[209] However, as noted above, tin was rarely shipped through Boston, although 89 pieces of tin worth £222 10s. were exported from Boston on 18 February 1467 by Edward IV's factor.[210] Similarly, the alien trade in pewter vessels rarely appears in Boston's enrolled customs accounts. The 15 lbs of tin and 34 lbs of pewter vessels valued at 16s. 6d. in 1507–8, the set of pewter vessels valued at 32s. in 1510–11, and two sets worth 40s. in 1511–12 are thus very much the exception and, even then, were of minor significance compared with the large amounts of pewter being shipped through London, Southampton and the ports of the south-west in this period.[211] Exports of pewter

206 Ormrod, 'The origins of tunnage and poundage', p. 216.
207 T.N.A., E356/5; E356/12; E356/13.
208 T.N.A., E356/5; E356/18.
209 Jenks, *Enrolled Customs Accounts*, Part 6, p. iv.
210 T.N.A., E122/10/7, f. 12d.
211 T.N.A., E356/24, mm. 9, 10d.; Schanz, *Englische Handelspolitik*, II, pp. 118–25.

by denizens were liable to poundage but, since they were not liable to the higher rate of poundage introduced in 1454, there was no reason to distinguish them in the enrolled customs accounts. Similarly, as Hansards were not liable to poundage in this period, the enrolled accounts do not include separate figures for their pewter exports. Thus, although we can see Hanseatic merchants exporting pewter in the particular accounts, as in 1488 when John Lewe paid custom on pewter valued at 20s., in the enrolled accounts this trade was included only within the total value of alien goods subject to the 1303 custom of 3d. in the pound.[212]

Figure 9.1 gives the total value of imports and exports valued for poundage at Boston between 1347 and 1548. Unfortunately, the many changes during this period in the categories of merchants and in the commodities which were liable to poundage tend to render the use of the returns of this subsidy 'both tedious and hazardous' for those wishing to interpret the significance of annual fluctuations in the value of goods on which it was levied.[213] The early grants of poundage, such as that collected in 1371–72, make it clear that it was to be levied on 'all goods and wares imported and exported except wools, hides and woolfells' and that no specific groups of merchants were exempt from paying it.[214] This meant, as can be seen in the surviving particular accounts for the late fourteenth and early fifteenth centuries, that Hanseatic merchants initially paid this subsidy on their imports and exports, including those of woollen cloth, worsted and wax.[215] Indeed, in December 1384, Hansards were accused (wrongly, it eventually transpired) of having delayed their arrival in the port of Boston until after Michaelmas 1384, when a grant of poundage expired, in order to avoid paying the subsidy.[216] However, in the mid-fifteenth century, strained relations between England and the Hanseatic League made the situation with regard to poundage much more complex. In 1437 the Hansards were freed from paying tunnage and poundage, but these subsidies were re-imposed on them from 29 September 1447. Then, from 2 October 1449, they were again exempted, although this exemption did not apply to the merchants of Lübeck (who dominated Boston's Hanseatic trade) and of Danzig. From September 1453 onwards, all Hansards were again to pay the subsidy but from April 1454 they were exempted once more, although again with the exception of the merchants of Lübeck, whose freedom from poundage was only restored from 14 February 1456.[217]

212 T.N.A., E122/11/4, f. 2v.

213 Carus-Wilson, *Overseas Trade of Bristol*, p. 12.

214 *Calendar of Fine Rolls, 1368–77*, pp. 141, 151.

215 See, for instance, T.N.A., E122/7/17; E122/7/19; E122/7/20; E122/7/21; E122/7/24; E122/7/27; E122/7/30; E122/7/30A; E122/8/6; E122/212/3.

216 *Calendar of Close Rolls, 1381–85*, pp. 501, 619–20.

217 Jenks, *Enrolled Customs Accounts*, Part 6, pp. v–vi; Jenks, *Enrolled Customs Accounts*, Part 9, pp. vii–xiii; Fudge, *Cargoes, Embargoes and Emissaries*. See also J. L. Bolton, 'Alien Merchants

Denizen merchants were also liable to the subsidy of poundage. As the particular accounts for the late fourteenth and early fifteenth centuries confirm, they initially paid this subsidy on their cloth exports.[218] However, as we saw above (in section 2.8), denizens were freed from paying tunnage and poundage in 1422–5, 1427–8, 1429 and 1436–7. In some cases, they were also freed from paying poundage on their cloth exports even when they remained liable to the subsidy on other goods, as they were for a year from 11 November 1426, for a year from 4 April 1428, and from 12 January 1431 to 13 January 1434. After 1 April 1437, denizens were permanently exempted from poundage on their cloth exports, but they continued to be liable for this subsidy on their other miscellaneous imports and exports and, perhaps surprisingly, even on their exports of worsted, even though these were also charged with the 1347 cloth custom.[219]

Unlike the Hansards, other aliens paid poundage throughout this period and, as the particular accounts for the late fifteenth century show, they remained liable to this subsidy on their cloth exports even after Hanseatic and denizen cloth exports had been exempted from it.[220] The only exception to this before 1539 was that made for the merchants of Veere (or 'Caumfer'), in Zeeland, who were granted exemption from poundage from December 1471 until the end of Edward IV's reign.[221] As a result, a number of the enrolled accounts for Boston either specify the value of the goods imported or exported by merchants of Veere which had not been charged with the subsidy, or at least state that the total value of the goods on which poundage had been paid did not include imports and exports of the men of Veere (see the notes to Figure 9.1). Finally, as we have seen (in section 2.6), in the seven years from 1539, alien merchants were allowed to pay customs and subsidies at the same rate as denizen merchants, which meant that they were exempt from poundage on their cloth exports. However, the enrolled accounts continued to specify the value of the small amounts of cloth exported by aliens which were exempted from poundage during this period. These have been included in the totals of goods valued for poundage in Figure 9.1.[222]

The frequent changes in the goods and merchants liable to poundage make it pointless to compare the total values of goods liable to poundage in the late fourteenth and early fifteenth centuries, when Hanseatic imports and exports and

---

in England in the reign of Henry VI' (unpublished University of Oxford B.Litt. thesis, 1971), pp. 29–30.

218 T.N.A., E122/7/17; E122/7/19; E122/7/20; E122/7/21; E122/7/2; E122/7/27; E122/7/30; E122/7/30A; E122/8/6; E122/212/3.

219 Jenks, *Enrolled Customs Accounts*, Part 6, pp. iv–v; T.N.A., E122/10/7, f. 15.

220 See, for instance, T.N.A., E122/7/24; Rigby, *Overseas Trade of Boston*, pp. 163, 167–8. For the late fifteenth century, see T.N.A., E122/10/1; E122/10/5; E122/10/14.

221 Jenks, *Enrolled Customs Accounts*, part 9, p.v. See footnote 123, above.

222 T.N.A., E356/27, mm. 4–6.

denizen cloth exports were being charged with the subsidy, with those later in the century when these goods were exempt. For instance, for the period from 12 April to 29 September 1413, the Boston collectors accounted for poundage collected on £4,511 18s. 10d. of imports and exports. However, as their particular account shows, 50% of this total was actually made up of denizen and Hanseatic cloth exports, i.e. of goods which were to be exempted from the subsidy later on in the century.[223] Similarly, from 2 December 1383 to Michaelmas 1384, cloth exports comprised almost 50% of the goods valued for poundage.[224] Thus, although there was a genuine decline of the miscellaneous trade in Boston over the course of the fifteenth century, this decline is greatly exaggerated by the eventual disappearance of denizen and Hanseatic cloth from the poundage returns. Presenting the figures for this trade in graph form would therefore give an extremely misleading impression of the fluctuations in this branch of the port's trade.

Similarly, the fact that cloth exports by non-Hanseatic alien merchants remained liable to poundage throughout this period means that it is futile to compare the total value of trade liable to poundage in Boston with that in other ports, where the amount of cloth exported by non-Hanseatic aliens was much greater. For instance, a mere seven cloths exported by non-Hanseatic aliens were valued for poundage at Boston in the year from Michaelmas 1500, whereas at London over 10,000 cloths were exported by non-Hanseatic merchants at this time.[225] Totals for the value of goods liable to poundage drawn from Boston's enrolled accounts are given in Figure 9.1 below, but these reservations should be borne in mind when interpreting their significance.

Whilst the total amounts collected for poundage recorded in the enrolled accounts can give a misleading impression of the fluctuations of Boston's miscellaneous trade in the later Middle Ages, the particular accounts for the subsidy are useful in providing us with an impression of the range of goods imported and exported by denizen merchants (for the alien miscellaneous trade, see section 2.6). By the late fourteenth century, denizens exported little but wool and cloth from Boston. From 2 December 1383 to Michaelmas 1384, for instance, denizen miscellaneous exports (excluding the value of cloth exports) amounted to only £88 of calfskins, butter, hose and linen, compared with over £3,200 of imports. Around a third of these imports was comprised of 'Prussian merchandise' brought from the Baltic, including osmund and copper from Sweden, furs, pitch, tar, timber, rye and Prussian canvas. Yet, despite the expansion of English merchants into the Baltic trade in this period, goods shipped from the Low Countries were the main source of denizen miscellaneous imports at this time. Particularly important were the raw materials used in England's growing textile industry, including dyestuffs, especially woad

223 T.N.A., E122/212/3.
224 T.N.A., E122/7/17.
225 Carus-Wilson and Coleman, *England's Export Trade*, p. 112.

(used for making Coventry 'blues') and madder, along with some litmus as well as alum, which was used as a mordant for fixing dyes. Also significant were soap and canvas, with the latter being used for sailcloth and for packing wool. In addition, a wide range of other goods was imported from the Low Countries, including copperware from Dinant, Spanish and Hungarian iron, linen, garlic and onions.[226]

By the late fifteenth and early sixteenth centuries, Boston's denizen miscellaneous trade, particularly that in imports, presents us with a very different picture from that in Richard II's reign. Exports, as before, were on a very minor scale, being valued at only £3 in 1466–7, £194, in 1486–7, £45 in 1489–90, £16 in 1522–3, and £30 in 1531–2, and were made up of tallow, calf- and lamb-skins, butter, beef, grain and legumes, along with small amounts of lead and sea-coal.[227] By contrast, the volume and nature of denizen imports had changed dramatically: whereas they amounted to over £3,200 in the ten months from December 1383, they were worth only £69 in 1466–7, £297 in 1486–7, £85 in 1489–90, £139 in 1522–3, and £498 in 1531–2.[228] 'Prussian' goods, such as osmund, canvas, timber and furs, were now rarely imported; when they were, they were usually shipped alongside goods from the Low Countries rather than coming directly from the Baltic. As before, goods brought from the Low Countries continued to dominate the denizen miscellaneous import trade, but these imports were no longer comprised of dyestuffs, soap and canvas. Rather, as was also the case with alien miscellaneous imports (see section 2.6), the denizen trade was now largely made up of Dutch herring, particularly salted herring, which accounted for 64 % of denizen miscellaneous imports in 1466–7 and 69 % in 1522–3.[229] In addition, a wide range of other goods was imported or re-exported from the Low Countries, including foodstuffs, such as garlic, onions and hops, and manufactured goods including hampers, earthen jars and paving tiles. Nevertheless, such goods were of little total value. In 1531–2, for instance, whilst denizens shipped linen, trenchers, nails, shovels, drinking pots, caps, combs, glass, gloves, paper and leather belts to Boston, these manufactured items made up only 6 % of denizen imports.[230]

Figure 9.1 Value of imports and exports liable to poundage at Boston, 1347–1548.

	£			£	
15.3.1347–26.11.1347	4552		1.11.1371–1.11.1372	15097	
28.2.1350–28.6.1350	839		16.11.1378–27.5.1379	10172	
24.9.1350–28.9.1351	6640		2.12.1383–Mich.1384	9720	

226 T.N.A., E122/7/17; E122/8/25.
227 T.N.A., E122/10/7; E122/11/2; E122/11/4; E122/12/10; E122/12/3.
228 T.N.A., E122/7/17; E122/10/7; E122/11/2; E122/11/4; E122/12/10; E122/12/3.
229 T.N.A., E122/10/7; E122/12/3.
230 T.N.A., E122/12/10.

	£	
24.11.1386–28.11.1387	20804	
20.3.1388–29.7.1388	4860	
29.7.1388–24.6.1389	19351	
24.6.1389–2.2.1390	8376	
1.3.1390–30.11.1390	13583	
30.11.1390Mich.1391	10477	
Mich.1391–Mich.1392	16297	
Mich.1392–Mich.1393	12921	
Mich.1393–Mich.1394	10689	
Mich.1394–Mich.1395	14058	
Mich.1395–Mich.1396	15934	
Mich.1396–Mich.1397	15806	
Mich.1397–Mich.1398	12370	
Mich.1398–15.9.1399	16299	
3.4.1401–25.6.1402	23576	
25.6.1402–15.4.1403	10686	
3.4.1403–Mich.1403	6493	
Mich.1403–Mich.1404	10019	
Mich.1404–Mich.1405	8547	
Mich.1405–Mich.1406	12812	
Mich.1406–Mich.1407	13413	
Mich.1407–Mich.1408	9607	
Mich.1408–Mich.1409	10636	
Mich.1409–Mich.1410	10247	
Mich.1410–Mich.1411	8758	
Mich.1411–Mich.1412	7948	
Mich.1412–Mich.1413	11365	
Mich.1413–Mich.1414	4608	
Mich.1414–Mich.1415	2486	
Mich.1415–Mich.1416	4920	
Mich.1416–Mich.1417	9368	
Mich.1417–Mich.1418	9751	
Mich.1418–Mich.1419	9150	
Mich.1419–10.10.1420	10488	
10.10.1420–Mich.1421	11043	
Mich.1421–31.8.1422	10409	
1.9.1422–Mich.1423	5874	Aliens only
Mich.1423–Mich.1424	6401	Aliens only
Mich.1424–Mich.1425	5979	Aliens only

	£	
1.8.1425–Mich.1425	128	Denizens only
Mich.1425–Mich.1426	8344	
Mich.1426–Mich.1427	6718	
Mich.1427–Mich.1428	136	Aliens only
Mich.1427–17.11.1427	24	Denizens only
4.4.1428–4.4.1429	1258	Denizens only
Mich.1428–1.11.1429	491	Aliens only
1.11.1429–1.11.1430	3891	
1.11.1430–20.10.1431	1345	
20.10.1431–Mich.1432	1660	
Mich.1432–Mich.1433	1906	
Mich.1433–Mich.1434	3443	
Mich.1434–Mich.1435	4015	
Mich.1435–10.10.1436	1801	
10.10.1436–11.11.1437	1110	
11.11.1437–Mich.1438	838	
Mich.1438–Mich.1439	840	
Mich.1439–Mich.1440	980	
Mich.1440–30.6.1441	618	
30.6.1441–Mich.1442	912	
Mich.1442–12.8.1443	665	
12.8.1443–12.10.1444	1346	
12.10.1444–12.10.1445	1107	
12.10.1445–24.6.1446	538	
24.6.1446–18.7.1447	1764	
18.7.1447–21.11.1448	863	
21.11.1448–21.11.1449	609	
21.11.1449–Mich.1450	960	
Mich.1450–3.2.1452	1129	
3.2.1452–Mich.1452	488	
Mich.1452–Mich.1453	980	
Mich.1453–Mich.1454	62	
Mich.1454–10.10.1455	196	
10.10.1455–10.10.1456	1483	note 1
10.10.1456–Mich.1457	127	
Mich.1457–Mich.1458	455	
Mich.1458–15.12.1459	No returns	
15.12.1459–1.9.1460	82	

	£	
1.9.1460–Mich.1461	326	note 2
Mich.1461–Mich.1462	277	
Mich.1462–20.7.1463	1742	note 3
20.7.1463–3.5.1464	55	
3.5.1464–25.2.1465	110	
25.2.1465–Mich.1465	293	
Mich.1465–25.3.1466	478	
25.3.1466–25.3.1467	622	note 4
25.3.1467–6.3.1468	761	note 5
6.3.1468–25.12.1468	408	
25.12.1468–Mich.1469	567	
Mich.1469–13.11.1470	255	note 6
26.10.1470–Mich.1471	266	note 7
Mich.1471–8.10.1472	323	note 8
8.10.1472–8.10.1473	133	note 9
8.10.1473–2.11.1474	58	note 10
2.11.1474–Mich.1475	200	note 11
Mich.1475–Mich.1476	449	note 12
Mich.1476–Mich.1477	489	note 13
Mich.1477–Mich.1478	336	note 14
Mich.1478–Mich.1479	407	note 15
Mich.1479–Mich.1480	546	
Mich.1480–Mich.1481	502	note 16
Mich.1481–Mich.1482	550	note 17
Mich.1482–Mich.1483	366	note 18
Mich.1483–Mich.1484	294	
Mich.1484–Mich.1485	416	
Mich.1485–Mich.1486	533	
Mich.1486–Mich.1487	520	
Mich.1487–Mich.1488	177	
Mich.1488–Mich.1489	372	
Mich.1489–Mich.1490	314	
Mich.1490–Mich.1491	273	
Mich.1491–Mich.1492	148	
Mich.1492–Mich.1493	425	
Mich.1493–Mich.1494	145	note 19
Mich.1494–Mich.1495	335	note 20
Mich.1495–Mich.1496	217	
Mich.1496–Mich.1497	360	

	£	
Mich.1497–Mich.1498	373	
Mich.1498–Mich.1499	358	
Mich.1499–Mich.1500	726	
Mich.1500–Mich.1501	862	
Mich.1501–Mich.1502	669	
Mich.1502–Mich.1503	1072	
Mich.1503–Mich.1504	1158	
Mich.1504–Mich.1505	342	
Mich.1505–Mich.1506	312	
Mich.1506–Mich.1507	604	
Mich.1507–Mich.1508	865	
Mich.1508–Mich.1509	317	
Mich.1509–Mich.1510	578	
Mich.1510–Mich.1511	469	
Mich.1511–Mich.1512	517	
Mich.1512–Mich.1513	140	
Mich.1513–Mich.1514	393	
Mich.1514–Mich.1515	649	
Mich.1515–Mich.1516	608	
Mich.1516–Mich.1517	553	
Mich.1517–Mich.1518	724	
Mich.1518–Mich.1519	862	
Mich.1519–Mich.1520	991	
Mich.1520–Mich.1521	1105	
Mich.1521–Mich.1522	207	
Mich.1522–Mich.1523	370	
Mich.1523–Mich.1524	454	
Mich.1524–Mich.1525	554	
Mich.1525–Mich.1526	495	
Mich.1526–Mich.1527	557	
Mich.1527–Mich.1528	576	
Mich.1528–Mich.1529	412	
Mich.1529–Mich.1530	642	
Mich.1530–Mich.1531	550	
Mich.1531–Mich.1532	805	
Mich.1532–Mich.1533	407	
Mich.1533–Mich.1534	777	
Mich.1534–Mich.1535	855	
Mich.1535–Mich.1536	819	

	£			£	
Mich.1536–Mich.1537	382		Mich.1542–Mich.1543	262	
Mich.1537–Mich.1538	549		Mich.1543–Mich.1544	227	
Mich.1538–Mich.1539	1075		Mich.1544–Mich.1545	466	
Mich.1539–Mich.1540	764		Mich.1545–Mich.1546	69	
Mich.1540–Mich.1541	1542		Mich.1546–Mich.1547	1542	
Mich.1541–Mich.1542	1124		Mich.1547–Mich.1548	1456	

(Source: T.N.A., E356 Enrolled customs accounts)

Notes to Figure 9.1:

- Note 1. Including £1138 of Hanseatic goods.
- Note 2. Including £49 10s. of denizen cloth and £226 5s. of Hanseatic cloth and coverlets.
- Note 3. Including £1,378 2s. of Hanseatic goods.
- Note 4. Including £254 of exports of the king's cloth and £470 16s. 8d. of Hanseatic goods after 24 June.
- Note 5. Including £388 11s. 8d. of Hanseatic goods.
- Note 6. Dates as in the enrolled account.
- Note 7. Dates as in the enrolled account.
- Note 8. Excluding £18 of goods liable to poundage of the merchants of Veere.
- Note 9. Excluding £347 of goods liable to poundage of the merchants of Veere.
- Note 10. Excluding £443 of goods liable to the new custom of 3d. in the pound, and exports of 193 clothes without grain of the merchants of Veere upon which poundage would normally have been paid.
- Note 11. Including £42 of Hanseatic goods, but excluding any miscellaneous goods and exports of 169½ cloths without grain of the merchants of Veere upon which poundage would normally have been paid.
- Note 12. Excluding £163 7s. of miscellaneous goods, and the export of 1 cloth without grain by merchants of Veere, who would normally have paid poundage.
- Note 13. Excluding £389 9s. 4d. of miscellaneous goods of the merchants of Veere upon which poundage would normally have been paid.
- Note 14. Excluding any miscellaneous goods and 6½ cloths without grain of the merchants of Veere upon which poundage would normally have been paid.
- Note 15. Excluding any miscellaneous goods and exports of 21 cloths without grain of the merchants of Veere upon which poundage would normally have been paid.
- Note 16. Excluding any miscellaneous goods of the merchants of Veere upon which poundage would normally have been paid.
- Note 17. Excluding any miscellaneous goods and exports of 7½ cloths without grain of the merchants of Veere upon which poundage would normally have been paid.

- Note 18. Excluding any miscellaneous goods and exports of 55 cloths without grain of the merchants of Veere upon which poundage would normally have been paid.
- Note 19. Excluding £41 13s. 4d. of Hanseatic goods.
- Note 20. Excluding £40 18s. 5½d. of Hanseatic goods.

3.

Conclusion: the transformation and decline of Boston's overseas trade, 1279–1548

The Exchequer customs accounts are an unrivalled source for the study of Boston's history in the later Middle Ages, and yet it is possible for the very richness of their detail to obscure the general and long-term trends in the port's commerce. What the enrolled accounts reveal, above all, is the long-term decline which all the branches of the port's trade underwent in the later Middle Ages. At the start of the fourteenth century, Boston possessed a prominence in England's overseas commerce which it was never to enjoy again, being second only to London in many branches of its trade. At this time, Boston's wool trade and its fair were at their peak, attracting alien merchants who brought a range of imports from a huge area: from Scandinavia and the Baltic, through the Low Countries to Gascony and Italy. By the end of the century, the port's alien trade had been transformed. The waning of St Botolph's fair, the decline of alien wine and cloth imports and salt exports, the government-introduced control of wool exports by English merchants, and the shift of the Italian wool trade to London and Southampton meant that by 1400, merchants from Gascony, Italy and the Low Countries played only minor role in the port's alien trade, which was now dominated by Hanse exports of woollen cloth and by imports of stockfish from the Hansards' Bergen *kontor*. The fifteenth century then witnessed the decline of the Hanseatic trade at Boston, as 'Esterlings' shifted their trade to London, where the merchants of Cologne had always concentrated their activities. By the early sixteenth century, their place in Boston had been taken by men from Holland and Zeeland, although their imports of salted herring could never compensate for the disappearance of the Hanseatic commerce from the port.

Nor did the trade of English merchants at Boston make up for the loss of Hanseatic imports and exports. In the late fourteenth century, the denizen wool trade at Boston initially remained buoyant, even though the total volume of wool exports was in decline. The denizen trade with the Baltic and, in particular, with the Low Countries was also lucrative in this period. Cloth exports by denizens from Boston were growing in the second half of the fourteenth century, although they were already overshadowed by those from Lynn, Hull and Southampton, let alone from Bristol and London. The growth of the cloth industry also stimulated the trade in imported dyestuffs. In the fifteenth century, however, as cloth came to replace raw wool as England's main export, Boston's wool trade inevitably declined even further. Its denizen cloth exports, like those of the Hansards, also dwindled as the London–Antwerp commercial axis began to dominate England's commerce. The wine trade also moved to the capital and the ports of the south-west and so, by the early sixteenth century, the trade of both denizen and alien merchants at Boston was chiefly comprised of imports of salted herring.

Unfortunately, the Exchequer customs accounts do not include coastal trade. Nonetheless, whilst it would be wrong to judge a port's fortunes simply by its overseas trade, it seems unlikely that a growth in coastal trade compensated for the decline in the volume of Boston's overseas trade.[231] Whilst Boston remained as a regional centre and the only town of any size in one of the richest areas of Tudor England, it was no longer one of the leading ports in the country. Thus, whereas England's population in 1563 was probably at a similar level to that of 1377 (and may actually have been even larger), it is possible that Boston's population had declined by over a quarter between these dates.[232] Paradoxically, as the Stump rose ever higher, Boston sank ever lower down England's urban hierarchy.[233]

231 M. Kowaleski, *Local Markets and Regional Trade in Medieval Exeter* (Cambridge, 1995), pp. 225–32; Kowaleski, 'Port towns', pp. 480–1; O. Coleman, 'Trade and prosperity in the fifteenth century: some aspects of the trade of Southampton', *Economic History Review*, second series, 16 (1963–64), pp. 9–22, at 19–20; A. R. Bridbury, 'English provincial towns in the later Middle Ages', *Economic History Review*, 34 (1981), pp. 1–24, at 8; Rigby, '"Sore decay" and "fair dwellings"', pp. 53–4.

232 Broadberry *et al.*, *British Economic Growth*, pp. 20, 29; Rigby, 'Medieval Boston', pp. 22–7; Rigby, '"Sore decay" and "fair dwellings"', pp. 52–5.

233 For the suggestion that the building of the Stump was financed by the corporate wealth of Boston's guilds, see Monckton, '"The beste and fayrest of al Lincolnshire"', pp. 29, 46–8; B. Ayers, *The German Ocean: Medieval Europe Around the North* Sea (Sheffield, 2016), p. 125. For the wealth of the Boston guild of the Blessed Virgin Mary in the early sixteenth century, see R. N. Swanson, *Indulgences in Late Medieval England: Passports to Paradise?* (Cambridge, 2007), pp. 375–6, 424, 436–41.

Appendix

Particulars of account of the collectors of tunnage and poundage in Boston, 28 November 1386 to 28 November 1387 (T. N. A., E122/7/19).

This appendix gives the text of the particular account of the collectors of the subsidy of tunnage and poundage in Boston in the year from 28 November 1386 (T.N.A., Exchequer K. R. Customs Accounts, E122/7/19). This account has been chosen for the detailed picture it provides of the port's trade, since, although exports of wool, woolfells and hides were exempt from tunnage and poundage, the subsidy was paid at this date by denizen, Hanseatic and other alien merchants on all of their other imports and exports, including both Hanseatic shipments of wine, woollen cloth, worsted and wax and denizen exports of woollen cloth, which were eventually exempted from the subsidy (see sections 2.8 and 2.9, above). The subsidy had been granted to Richard II by the 'Wonderful Parliament', which met at Westminster in October 1386, to help towards the costs of the defence of the realm and the safekeeping of the sea (for the grant and the conditions attached to it, see *Rotuli Parliamentorum*, volume III, pp. 220–1; C. Given-Wilson, ed., 'Richard II: parliament of October 1386, text and translation', item 18, in Given-Wilson *et al.*, *Parliament Rolls of Medieval England*; *Calendar of Fine Rolls, 1383–91*, p. 169; N. Saul, *Richard II* (New Haven, 1997), p. 161; W. M. Ormrod, 'Government by commission: the continual council of 1386 and English royal administration', *Peritia*, 10 (1996), pp. 303–321). The subsidy was to be paid at the rate of three shillings per tun of wine and one shilling (twelve pence) in the pound on all other imports and exports except for wool, hides and woolfells.

Five documents relating to this subsidy survive for Boston for the year from 28 November 1386 and they are still contained in the leather pouch which originally held the account of the subsidy collectors and the rolls of the controllers. The eight membranes of which these five documents are comprised are numbered 3 to 10 in pencil in a modern hand (for an English translation of all five documents, see Rigby, *Overseas Trade of Boston*, pp. 54–77). The first document (m. 3) is a writ dated 28 November 1386 commissioning Robert Sutton and Gilbert Maghfeld to collect the subsidy in Boston by the controlment of John Stranshale (see *Calendar of Fine Rolls, 1383–91*, p. 169; *Calendar of Patent Rolls, 1385–9*, p.247); the writ commissioning Stranshale as controller has not survived. Sutton was a Lincoln merchant who traded via Boston (Rigby, *Overseas Trade of Boston*, pp. 232–9, 240–2; Rigby, '"John of Gaunt's Palace" and the Sutton family of Lincoln', pp. 35–9), whilst Maghfeld was a London merchant and alderman who also served as a customs collector in Southampton and London (Rigby, *Overseas Trade of Boston*, pp. 240–2; E. Rickert, 'Extracts from a fourteenth-century account book', *Modern Philology*, 24 (1926–27), pp. 111–19, 249–56; M. K. James, 'A London merchant of the fourteenth century', *Economic History Review*, second series, 8 (1955–56), pp. 364–76). Although Sutton and Maghfeld were also responsible for collecting the great and petty customs in Boston at this time, they compiled separate particular accounts for the subsidy of tunnage and poundage and for the other customs, which were then enrolled on two separate rolls at the Exchequer (T.N.A., E356/5, m. 25; E356/14).

The second document (m. 4) is a writ dated 24 December 1386 commissioning Richard Northwode to replace Stranshale as controller of the subsidy in Boston (see *Calendar of Patent Rolls, 1385–89*, p. 248); neither of these men was responsible for the great and petty customs in the port, for which Reginald Curteys was the controller during this period (T.N.A., E356/14). The third document (m. 5) is the roll of Master John Stranshale, who at this time was rector of St Botolph's parish church in Boston (Thompson, *The History and Antiquities of Boston*, p. 170), and was controller of the subsidy in Boston from 28 November to 24 December 1386. Unusually for a controller's roll, this account includes not only the value of the goods liable to poundage, but also the amount of subsidy due from them. The fourth document whose text is given below is the account of the Boston collectors Robert Sutton and Gilbert Maghfeld for the entire year from 28 November 1386. It is comprised of two membranes (mm. 6–7), sewn together at the head, Exchequer-style. The document first lists the ships importing goods into Boston (mm. 6–7) and then those carrying exports (m. 7d.). It gives details of the merchants and goods liable to subsidy on each ship and the amount of subsidy which was due. The final document in the pouch (mm. 8–10) is the roll of Richard Norwode (for whom, see Rigby, *Overseas Trade of Boston*, pp. 256–7), who was controller in Boston from 25 December 1386 until 28 November 1387. As in most controllers' rolls, only the values of goods are given, rather than the subsidy due from them, with the exception of two ships, in one of which the amount of subsidy to be paid was problematic (see note 17, below).

Since all merchants were required to pay tunnage and poundage at the same rates, the collectors did not need to distinguish denizen, Hanseatic and other alien merchants as such in their account (although, unusually, two of the listed merchants are specified as being denizens), as was necessary in their accounts of the petty custom. The ships listed in the account are identified by the name of their masters. No attempt was made to specify their homeports, even though a statute of 1381 which had ordained that the king's lieges should only load their imports and exports in ships of the king's allegiance should have provided an incentive for the homeports of ships to be recorded. This statute, whose purpose was to encourage the availability of ships for naval service, was still in force at the time of this account, although it had been qualified in 1382 by the concession that denizen merchants could use other ships if suitable native ones were not available (*Statutes of the Realm*, volume II (London, 1816), pp. 18, 28, 77). As a result of the collectors' failure to record the ships' homeports, the crown had no means of checking whether the statute was being observed. In practice, little effort seems to have been made to enforce this legislation, even though the customs collectors were reminded in 1398 about the need to put it into effect (*Calendar of Close Rolls, 1396–99*, p. 340). The Boston customs accounts of the early fifteenth century also failed to give the homeports of ships arriving at or leaving the port (T.N.A., E122/8/1; E122/8/2; E122/8/4; E122/8/6; E122/8/24; E122/8/25; E122/212/3); only from the second half of the century do the accounts systematically note such homeports (see, for instance, T.N.A. E122/10/1; E122/10/4; E122/10/5; E122/10/7; E122/10/8; E122/10/17; E122/10/20; E122/10/26). The particular customs accounts do not normally give the ports from which ships had arrived or to which they were bound, apart from noting ships leaving with wool for the Calais staple (see, for instance, T.N.A., E122/10/4; E122/10/5; E122/10/7; E122/10/8). However, in the account below, five ships laden with wheat are noted as having left for Bordeaux, with these entries probably being related to the requirement that ships leaving English ports for Gascony should first gather at Sandwich and then sail in convoy because of the threat posed by enemy attacks (*Calendar of Close Rolls, 1385–89*, pp. 257, 348).

Since we have the rolls of the two controllers of this subsidy in Boston for this period, we can compare the text of the collectors' account with that of the controllers' rolls. Overall, what is most striking are the similarities between the collectors' account and the rolls of the two controllers. For instance, of the entries for around 280 merchants listed as importing or exporting goods liable to tunnage and poundage in Boston during this period, only two do not appear in the same order in the controllers' rolls as that in the collectors' account (see note 243, below). Similarly, ships which arrived at or left the port on the same day are listed in the same order in both sources. The order in which the goods of individual merchants are listed sometimes differs between the collectors' account and the controller's rolls. There are also some minor discrepancies, such as the controller's roll saying that Conrad Johnson and the sailors on his ship had imported 'fish and boards', whereas the collectors' account has them as being liable to subsidy on 'osmund and fish'. Inevitably, there are differences of spelling between the collectors' account and the controllers' rolls, although the names of individuals are found in various forms even within the same account (as when Hertwicus 'Somme' in the collectors' account becomes Hertwicus 'Semne' in its later entries), and there are slips of transcription, as when 'De Reynero' in the collectors' account becomes 'De Rogero' in the controller's roll. However, in nearly every case, the actual values of the goods listed for each merchant and the subsidy which was due from them, which was after all, what the Exchequer was primarily interested in, are the same in both rolls. This suggests, as was noted above, either that one roll was based on the other, or that the two were drawn from a common source, probably that of a manifest provided by the shipmaster.

Significant differences between the collectors' account and the controllers' rolls are noted in the footnotes below, as are problematic entries. Abbreviated words have been extended. Editorial insertions within the text are indicated by square brackets.

m. 6.
Particule compoti Roberti Sutton et Gilberti Maghfeld, collectorum trium solidorum de dolio vini et duodecim denariis de libra in portu ville de Sancto Botulpho, videlicet de exitibus eiusdem subsidii a vicesimo octavo die Novembris anno x usque xxv diem[234] proximo sequentum per visum et testimonium Magistri Johannis Stranshall, contrarotulator eiusdem subsidii ibidem. Et ab eodem xxiiii die Decembris[235] anno x usque xxviii diem Novembris proximo sequentum anno xi, per visum et testimonium Ricardi Northwod de Sancto Botulpho, mercatoris, contrarotulator dicti subsidii ibidem.

Navis Johannis Wolf applicuit in portu de Sancto Botulpho vicesimo die Decembris anno regni regis Ricardi secundi decimo.
De eodem et marinariis suis pro iiii lastis allecis. Valor: xiii li. vi s. viii d. Subsidium: xiii s. iiii d.
De Laurentio Claisson pro iii lastis allecis. Valor: x li. Subsidium: x s.
De Rogero Harsyk pro xiiii lastis allecis: xlvi. li. xiii s. iiii d. Subsidium: xlvi s. viii d.
De Roberto Shepeleye pro x lastis allecis: xxxiii li. vi. s. viii d. Subsidium: xxxiii s. iiii d.
De Johanne Rye pro v lastis allecis. Valor: xvi li xiii s. iiii d. Subsidium: xvi s. viii d.
De Roberto Cleaundre pro v lastis allecis. Valor: xvi li. xiii s. iiii d. Subsidium: xvi s. viii d.
De Johanne de Leicestre pro iiii lastis. Valor: xiii li. vi. S. viii d. Subsidium: xiii s. iiii d.[236]
De Rogero Vyncent pro iiii lastis. Valor: xiii li. vi. s. viii d. Subsidium: xiiis. iiii d
De Ricardo Ayleward pro iii lastis dimidio, iiii barellis allecis. Valor: xii li. xiii s. iiii d. Subsidium: xii s. viii d.[237]
De Johanne Reede pro iiii lastis dimidio allecis. Valor: xv li. Subsidium: xv s.
De Johanne Roper pro viii barellis. Valor: liii s. iiii d. Subsidium: ii. s. viii d.
De Johanne Somoner pro i lasto, xv barellis allecis. Valor: vi li. Subsidium: vi s.
Summa valoris istius navis: ciiii^{xx}xix li. xiii s. iiii d. Subsidii: ix l. xix s. viiid.

Navis Willelmi Barthagh applicuit in portu predicto eodem die.
De eodem et marinariis suis pro vi lastis allecis: xx li. Subsidium: vi s.[238]

234 'Decembris' seems to have been omitted here.
235 The date given here is 24 December, even though Stranshale's term is said to have ended on 25 December in the previous line. The controllers' rolls give Stranshale's term as controller as ending on 24 December and Norwode's as starting on 25 December.
236 Here, and in many entries below, 'allecis' has been omitted in the account.
237 The controller's account omits 'iiii barellis'.
238 The controller's roll omits 'et marinariis'.

De Reynero filio Rogeri pro i barello dimidio allecis. Valor: viii s. iiii d. Subsidium: v d.[239]
De Ricardo Fransham pro vii lastis allecis. Valor: xxiii li. vi s. viii d. Subsidium: xxiii s. iiii d.
De Radulpho Pakker pro v lastis, vii barellis allecis. Valor: xviii li. xiii s. iiii d. Subsidium: xviii s. viii d.
De Johanne Appull pro iii lastis, vii barellis allecis. Valor: xii li. Subsidium: xii s.
De Rogero Vyncent pro for i lasto dimidio. Valor: c s. Subsidium: v s.
De Johanne Rye pro v lastis allecis. Valor: xvi li. xiii s. iiii d. Subsidium: xvi s. viiid.
De Johanne Abraham pro i lasto allecis. Valor lxvi s. viii d. Subsidium: iii s. iiii d.
De Ricardo Goldryng pro i lasto allecis. Valor: lxvi s. viii d. Subsidium: iii s. iiii d.
De Johanne Harsyk pro ii lastis, dimidio barello allecis: vi li. xvi s. viii d. Subsidium: vi. s x d.
De Willelmo Hubard pro xi barellis: lx s. Subsidium: 3s.
De Alano Whitebred pro i lasto, vii barellis. Valor: cvi s. viii d. Subsidium: v s. iiii d.[240]
Summa valoris istius navis: cxvii li. xviii s. iiii d. Subsidii: cxvii s. xi d.

Navis Conradi Johnson applicuit in portu predicto eodem die.
De eodem et marinariis suis pro osmondo et pisce. Valor: vi li. Subsidium: vi s.[241]
De Johanne Godfreye pro oleo. Valor: lxvi s. viii d. Subsidium: iii s. iiii d.
De Everardo Russenbergh pro oleo et pisce. Valor: lxxii li. vi. s. iiii d. Subsidium: lxxii s. iiii d.
De Henrico Croppelyng pro oleo et pisce. Valor: x l. xv s. Subsidium: x s. ix d.
De Bernardo Knoflok pro oleo et pisce. Valor: vi li. Subsidium: vi s.
De Johanne Holst pro oleo et pisce. Valor: xlvii li. vi s. Subsidium: xlvii s. iiii d.
De Johanne Calswyncle pro oleo et pisce. Valor: lxxi li. Subsidium: lxxi s.
De Alberto Brokeman pro oleo et pisce. Valor: xxi li. x s. Subsidium: xxi s. vi. d.
De Johanne Kalff pro oleo et pisce. Valor: xxvi li. iii s. Subsidium: xxvi s. ii d.
De Wynkino Brandebergh pro oleo et pisce. Valor: xviii li. xviii s. Subsidium: xviii s. xi d. q.
De Tidekinus Luchogh pro oleo et pisce. Valor: xxiii li. ii s. Sibsidium: xxiii s. i d. q.
De Johanne Sloter pro oleo et pisce. Valor: lxii li. xii s. viii d. Subsidium: lxii s. viii d.
De Johanne Gronogh pro oleo et pisce. Valor: xxiii li. iii. s. iiii d. Subsidium: xxiii s. ii d.
De Hermanno van Hale pro pisce. Valor: viii li. x. s. Subsidium: viii s. vi d.
De Johanne Reynesbergh pro oleo et pisce. Valor: xiiii li. xiiii s. Subsidium: xiiii s. viii d. ob.

239 The controller's roll gives this entry as 'De Rogero'.
240 The controller's roll gives this entry as 'De Willelmo Whittebreed'.
241 The controller's roll gives this entry as 'pro pisce et bordis'.

De Hermanno Mynne pro oleo et pisce. Valor: xv li. vii s. Subsidium: xv s. iiii d. q.
Suuma valoris istius navis: ccccxxx li. Subsidium: xxi li. x s. ix d.

Navis Laurentii Claisson applicuit ibidem eodem die.[242]
De marinariis suis pro vii lastis, ix barellis. Valor: xxvii li. x s. Subsidium: xxvii s. vi. d.
De Reginaldo Reede pro v lastis, v barellis. Valor: xviii li. Subsidium: xviii s.
De Johanne Appull pro iiii lastis, i barello. Valor: xiii li. xiii s. iiii d. Subsidium: xiii s. viii d.
De Willelmus Hubard pro ii lastis, viii barellis. Valor: ix l. Subsidium: ix s.
De Ricardo Ayleward pro vi lastis. Valor: xx li. Subsidium: xx s.
De Rogero Harsyk pro vi lastis. Valor: xx li. Subsidium: xx s.
De Johanne Roper pro iii lastis, iii barellis. Valor: x li. xiii s. iiid. Subsidium: x s. viii d.
De Johanne Rye pro iii lastis dimidio. Valor: xi li. xiii s. iiii d. Subsidium: xi s. viii d.
De Thoma Kiele pro xii lastis, iii barellis. Valor: xl li. xv s. vii d. Subsidium: xl s. ix d. ob.
De Nicholao Greene pro i lasto, xi barellis. Valor: vi l. ii s. iiii d. Subsidium: vi s. i d. ob.
De Johanne Somoner pro iii lastis. Valor: x li. Subsidium: x s.
De Thoma Porter pro ix lastis, v barellis. Valor: xxxi li x s. Subsidium: xxxi s. vi d.
De Johanne Leycestre pro v lastis, ii barellis. Valor: xvii li. iiii s. viii d. Subsidium: xvii s. iii d.
De Wessello Keklen pro viii barellis allecis. Valor: lii s. Subsidium: iis. vii d. q.
De Laurentio Claisson pro vi lastis dimidio. Valor: xxi li. xiii s. iiii d. Subsidium: xxi s. viii d.
De Waltero Cothom pro vii barellis. Valor: xl s. Subsidium: ii s.
De Johanne Abraham pro vi lastis allecis. Valor xx li. Subsidium: xx s.[243]
De Willelmo Barthagh pro i lasto allecis. Valor: lxvi s. viii d. Subsidium: iii s. iiii d.
De predicto Johanne Abraham pro i lasto heryngsmolt. Valor: iiii li. xiii s. iiii d. Subsidium: iiii s. viii d.
Summa valoris istius navis: cciiii^{xx}x li vii s. xi d. Subsidii: xiiii li. x s. ix d.

Navis Henrici Hoggester applicuit ibidem eodem die.
De edoem et marinariis suis pro bitumen et pisce. Valor: lviii s. Subsidium: ii s. xi d.[244]
De Johanne Godefray pro bitumen et oleo. Valor: l s. Subsidium: ii s. vi d.

242 The controller's roll gives this ship as arriving on 22 December, which would affect the date of arrival of the ship of Henry Hoggester, below.

243 The inversion of the names of Abraham and Barthagh in the controller's roll is the only difference in the order of the merchants' names listed in all of the ships in the controllers' and collectors' accounts. The controller's account wrongly gives Abraham as having one last of herring.

244 The controller's roll gives this entry as 'pro pisce et bordis'.

De Egbarto Ravensbergh pro ermyn, oleo et pisce. Valor: cxxxix li. vii s. Subsidium: vi li. xix s. v d.[245]
De Johanne van Hamell pro oleo et pisce. Valor: xlv li. x s. Subsidium: xlv. s. vi d.
De Ludekino Skepensted pro oleo, pisce et aliis: xxi li. v s. viii d. Subsidium: xxi s. iii d. ob.[246]
De Ernesto de Lubyk pro oleo et pisce. Valor: xxvii li. vii s. iiii d. Subsidium: xxvii s. iiii d. ob.
De Henrico van Olde pro oleo et pisce. Valor: xxiiii li. Subsidium: xxiiii s.
De Johanne Skromp pro oleo et pisce. Valor: xxix li. x s. Subsidium: xxix s. vi d.
De Alberto Brokeman pro oleo et pisce. Valor: xi li. Subsidium: xi s.
De Fulberto van Hyde pro oleo et pisce. Valor: li li. viii s. Subsidium: li s. v d. q.
De Hermanno van Hale pro oleo et pisce. Valor xii li. v s. Subsidium: xii s. iii d.
De Hillario Whitman pro et pisce. Valor: ix li. xii d. Subsidium: ix s. i d.
De Tidkino Lukhogh pro oleo et pisce. Valor: xxiii li. v s. Subsidium: xxiii s. iii d.
De Ludekino vanderHyde pro oleo et pisce: xlii li. vi d. Subsidium: xlii s. ob.
De Arnaldo vanderHell pro oleo et pisce: xx li. xvi s. Subslidium: xx s. x d.
De Johanne Sloter pro oleo et pisce. Valor: xli li. Subsidium: xli s.
De Bernardo Knoflok pro oleo et pisce. Valor: xli li. x s. Subsidium: xli s. vi d.
De Arnaldo Knowold pro oleo et pisce. Valor: xxiiii li. Subsidium: xxiiii s.[247]
De Hermanno Mynne pro oleo et pisce. Valor: iiii^{xx}ii li. Subsidium: iiii li. ii s.
De Henrico Yernhatt pro oleo et pisce. Valor: xxxvi li. x s. Subsidium: xxxvi s. vi d.
Summa valoris istius navis: Dciiii^{xx}vii li. iiis. vi. d. Subsidii: xxxiiii li. vii s. iiii d. ob. q. m. 6d.

Navis Johannis Abott applicuit iiii die Februarii.
De eodem et marinariis suis pro pisce. Valor: iiii^{xx}xiii li. Subsidium: iiii li. xiii s.
De Ludekyno van Heid pro pisce. Valor: cxvi li. Subsidium: cxvi s.
De Johanne Hamele pro pisce. Valor: iiii^{xx}ix li. Subsidium: iiii li. ix s.
De Henrico Etlagh pro pisce. Valor: c li. xix s. ii d. Subsidium: c s. xi d. ob.
De Lamberto van Wonne pro pisce. Valor: lxxii li. Subsidium: lxxii s.
Summa valoris istius navis: ccccIxx li. xix s. ii d. Subsidii: xxiii li. x s. xi d. ob

Navis Jacobi Suythwynd applicuit ibidem eodem di.
De eodem at marinariis suis pro pisce. Valor: ciiii^{xx} li. xvii s. iiii d. Subsidium: ix s. x d. ob.
De Johanne Crousynge pro pisce. Valor: clxv li. Subsidium: viii li. v s.
De Johanne Hamele pro pisce. Valor:iiii^{xx}x. Subsidium: iiii li. x s.
Bernardo Knoffelok pro pisce. Valor: cxx li. Subsidium: vi li.

245 The controller's roll gives this entry as 'pro pisce et oleo'.
246 The controller's roll gives this entry as 'pro pisce et oleo'.
247 The controller's roll gives this entry as 'De Arnaldo Sconewod'.

De Ludekyno Skyppenstedd pro pisce. Valor: iiii^{xx}xviii li. Subsidium: iiii li. xviii s.
Summa valoris istius navis: Dcliii li. xvii s. iiii d. Subsidii: xxxii li. xiii s. x d. ob.

Navis Hermanni Mynne applicuit ibidem eodem die.
De eodem et marinariis suis pro pisce. Valor: ciiii^{xx} li. vii s. vi d. Subsidium: ix li. iiii d. ob.
De Augustino van Grene pro pisce. Valor: clxvii li. Subsidium: viii li. vii s.
De Johanne Slotir pro pisce. Valor: iiii^{xxx}viii li. Subsidium: iiii li. xviiis.
De Johanne van Heide pro pisce. Valor: clxxi. Subsidium: viii li. xi s.
De Hertwico Somme pro pisce. Valor: xlv li. Subsidium: xlv s.
Summa valoris istius navis: Dclxi li. vii s. vi d. Subsidii: xxxiii li. xvi d. ob.

Navis Theobaldi Otenson applicuit ibidem eodem die.
De eodem et marinariis suis pro vii lastis dimido. Valor: xx li. xvi s. Subsidium: xx s. ix d. ob.
De Hermanno Staynford pro xi lastis. Valor: xxx li. Subsidium: xxx s.
De Reginaldo Reed pro xviii lastis dimidio. Valor: l li. Subsidium: l s.
De Everardo van Spryng pro xviii lastis. Valor: xlviii li. Subsidium: xlviii s.
Summa valoris istius navis: cxlviii li. xvi s. Subsidii: vii li. viii s. ix d. ob.

Navis Petri Petreson applicuit xvi die Februarii.
De eodem et marinariis suis pro for cepe et allio. Valor: xiiii li. x s. Subsidium: xiiii s. vi d.
Suuma valoris istius navis: paret. Subsidii: paret.

Navis Henrici Sounde applicuit ibidem eodem die.
De eodem et marinariis suis pro pisce. Valor: cxxviii li. viii s. Subsidium: vi li. viii s. iiii d. ob
De Johanne Svenerlyng pro pisce. Valor: cli li. Subsidium: vii li. xi s.
De Johanne Grove pro pisce. Valor: ccl li. Subsidium: xii li. x s.
De Johanne Gronough pro pisce. Valor: ciiii^{xx}xix li. Subsidium: ix li. xix s.
Summa valoris istius navis: Dccxxviii li. viii s. Subsidii: xxxvi li. viii s. iiii d. ob.

Navis Nicholai Fure applicuit ibidem eodem die.
De eodem et marinariis suis pro pisce. Valor: lxxvi li. xv s. v d. Subsidium: lxxvi s. ix d. q.
De Johanne Sternbergh pro pisce. Valor: ciiii^{xx}iiii. Subsidium: ix li. iiii s.
De Everardo Leuyngcamp pro pisce. Valor: cclxiiii. Subsidium: xiii li. iiii s.
De Alberto Brokeman pro pisce. Valor: iiii^{xx}xv li. Subsidium: iiii li. xv s.
Summa valoris istius navis: Dcxix li. xv s. v d. Subsidii: xxx li. xix s. ix d. q.

Navis Johannis Pollerman applicuit eodem die.
De eodem et marinariis suis pro nucibus et all': xix li ii s. iiii d. Subsidium: xix s. i d. ob.[248]
De Johanne Keklen pro asseris et madre. Valor: xxxiii li. Subsidium: xxxiii s.
Summa valoris istius navis: lii li. ii s. iiii d. Subsidii: lii s. i d. ob.

Navis Henrici Keller applicuit eodem die.
De eodem et marinariis suis pro nucibus et all'. Valor: xii li. iiii s. Subsidium: xii s. ii d. ob.
De eodem [sic] Hermanno Braught pro osmondo. Valor: lx li. Subsidium: lx s.
Summa valoris istius navis: lxxii li. iiii s. Subsidiim: lxxii s. ii d. ob.

Navis Bartholomei Martynson applicuit ibidem eodem die.
De eodem et marinariis suis pro anguilla salsa. Valor: xv s. iiii d. Subsidium: ix d. q.
Summa valoris: paret. Subsidii: paret.

Navis Egidii Martynson applicuit xix die Februarii.
De Nicholao atte Green pro allecis. Valor: xli li. iii s. iiii d. Subsidium: xli s. ii d.
De eodem pro ii doliis et i pipa vini. Subsidium: vii s. vi d.
Summa valoris istius navis: paret. Subsidii: paret.
Summa doliorum vini: paret. Subsidii: paret.

Navis Segbaldi Fure applicuit xi die Martii.
De eodem pro allecis. Valor: xxvi s. viii d. Subsidium: xvi d.[249]
Summa: paret. Subsidii: paret.

Navis Petri Lamb applicuit primo die Aprilis.
De eodem at marinariis suis pro all'. Valor: liiii s. viii d. Subsidium: ii s. ix d.
Summa valoris: paret. Subsidii: paret.

Navis Adelini Clote applicuit ibiden eodem die.
De eodem et marinariis suis pro panno lineo. Valor: c s. Subsidium: v s.
De Hermanno Braught pro osmondo. Valor: cvi s. viii d. Subsidium: v s. iiii d.

---

248 The abbreviation here is 'all'', as it is in the controller's roll, which usually refers to garlic (allium or alleum) but can also, as in the case of the entry for John Rode on the ship of Herman Growell below, be used for herring (allecium), even though the latter is usually abbreviated as 'allec'' and is usually, but not always, specified as being in lasts or barrels. The large value here, as in some of the other entries for 'all'' below, may suggest that herring rather than garlic is meant.

249 This entry is given as 'pro all'' in the collectors' roll but is specified in the controller's roll as being for 'allecium' (herring) rather than for 'allium' (garlic).

De eodem pro xii doliis vini de reno. Subsidium: xxxvi s.
Summa valoris istius navis: x li. vi s. viii d. Subsidii: x s. iiii d.
Summa doliorum vini: paret. Subsidii: paret.

Navis Petri de Kent applicuit ibidem xiiii die Maii.
De Roberto Chamberlein pro vii barellis olei. Valor: lvi s. viii d. Subsidium: ii s. x d.
De Johanne Abraham pro osmondo. Valor: viii li. xviii s. Subsidium: viii s. xi d. ob.
Summa valoris istius navis: xi li. xv s. iiii d. Subsidii: xi s. ix d. ob.

Navis Hermanni Mynne applicuit ibidem xxviii die Maii.
De eodem et marinarris suis pro pisce. Valor iiii^{xx}xiiii li. ix s. vi. d. Subsidium: iiii li. xiiii s. v d. ob. q.
De Johanne Papen pro pisce. Valor: cxliiii. Subsidium: vii li. iiii s.
De Tidekyno Luchogh pro pisce. Valor: $ciiii^{xx}$ii. Subsidium: ix li. ii s.
De Hermanno Cok pro pisce. Valor: clxvii li. Subsidium: viii li. vii s.
De Wynkino Brambergh pro pisce. Valor: xxii. Subsidium: xxii s.
Summa valoris istius navis: Dcix li. ix s. vi d. Subsidii: xxx li. ix s. v d. ob. q.

Navis Johannis Weste applicuit ibidem ultimo die Maii.
De Johanne Harold pro bordis et osmondo. Valor: xxxii s. Subsidium: xix d. ob.
De Johanne Daubenaye pro osmondo. Valor: xvii li. Subsidium: xvii s.
Summa valoris istius navis: xviii li xii s. Subsidii: xviii s. vii d. ob.

m. 7.
Navis Martini Williamson applicuit primo die Julii.
De Roberto Chamberlein pro anguilla salsa. Valor: liiii li. Subsidium: liii s.
Summa valoris istius navis: paret . Subsidii: paret.

Navis Segbaldi Fure applicuit ibidem ix die Julii.
De eodem et marinariis suis pro bordis. Valor: xvii li. iii s. vi. d. Subsidium: xvii s. ii d. q.
Summa valoris istius: paret. Subsidii: paret.

Navis Laurentii Clayson applicuit ibidem xxvi die Julii.
De eodem et marinariis suis pro xliii doliis vini. Subsidium: vi li. ix s.
De Petro Gernon pro xxx doliis vini. Subsidium: iiii li. x s.
De Willelmo French pro xxiiii doliis vini. Subsidium: lxxii s.
De Willelmo Warde pro xxx doliis. Subsidium: iiii li. x s.
Summa doliorum istius navis: cxxviii dolia. Subsidii: xix li. i s.[250]

---

250 The first entry for this ship was originally given as being for 44 tuns of wine, as it appears in the controller's roll, but this was then corrected to 43 tuns. The amount of subsidy given

Navis Rogeri atte Hous applicuit ibidem eodem die.
De eodem et marinariis suis pro xlvii doliis vini, i pipa. Subsidium: vii li. ii s. vi d.
Summa doliorum istius navis: paret. Subsidii: paret.

Navis Johannis Sell applicuit xxviii die Julii.
De eodem et marinariis suis [pro] madre. Valor: xxvii li. Subsidium: xxvii s.
De Willelmo French pro rosyn. Valor: lx s. Subsidium: iii s.
De Alano Tork pro ferro. Valor: xxvi s. x d. Subsidium: xvi d. ob.
Summa valoris istius navis: xxxi li. vi s. x d. Subsidii: xxxi s. iiii d. ob.

Navis Johnannis Wolf applicuit ibidem ultimo die Augusti.
De eodem et marinariis suis pro all'. Valor: xlviii li. ii s. vii d. Subsidium: xlviii s. i d. ob. q.
De Johanne Appull pro osmondo. Valor: ciiii^{xx}xi li. xv s. Subsidium: ix li. xi s. ix d.
De Henrico Kerle pro wadda. Valor: cclxxix li. v s. Subsidium: xiii li. xix s. iii d.
De Thoma Lach[eberi] pro smigmate. Valor: ciiii^{xx}xviii li. xv s. Subsidium: ix li. xviii s. ix d.[251]
De Roberto Cleaundre pro madre. Valor: clxi li. xv s. Subsidium: viii li xxi d.
Summa valoris istius navis: Dccclxxix li. xii s. vii d. Subsidii: xliii li. xix s. vii d. ob. q.

Navis Adriani Pierson applicuit eodem die.
De Frederico de Flete pro all'. Valor: xxxii li. ii s. Subsidium: xxxii s. i d. q.
De Waltero Pescodd pro alom. Valor: xx li. xvi s. Subsidium: xx s. ix d. ob. q.
Summa valoris istius navis: lii li xviii s. Subsidii: lii s. xi d.

Navis Hermanni Pilch applicuit ibidem eodem die.
De Johanne Harsyk pro ferro. Valor: cxvi li. xii d. Subsidium: cxvi s. i d.
De Thoma Lach[eberi] pro osmondo. Valor: xxxiii li. xiii s. iiii d. Subsidium: xxxiii s. viii d.
Summa valoris istius navis: cxlix li. xiiii s. iiii d. Subsidii: vii li. ix s. ix d.

Navis Simonis de Westvale applicuit ibidem eodem die.
De eodem pro pisce. Valor: cciiii^{xx}xviii li. xii s. x d. Subsidium: xiiii li. xviii s. viii d.

---

here is that due for 43 tuns, but the controller's roll (which, unusually, lists the amounts of subsidy due from the merchants on this ship) gives the tunnage due from 44 tuns. The total amount of wine on this ship is given by the collectors as an uncorrected 128 tuns, but a marginal entry notes that this should read 127 tuns, to allow for the reduction of the first entry from 144 to 143 tuns.

251 Lacheberi's name is given in the abbreviated form of 'Lach' in this account, but has been extended here and below from references in other accounts (see the index entry for him in Rigby, *Overseas Trade of Boston*, p. 292).

De Johanne Kekle pro wadda. Valor: cclxxix li. xv s. Subsidium: xiii li. xix s. ix d.
De Johanne van Ler pro cera. Valor: lxv li. xv s. Subsidium: lxv s. ix d.
Summa valoris istius navis: Dcxliiii li. ii s. x d. Subsidii: xxxii li. iiii s. ii d.

Navis Johannis Pollerman applicuit ibidem eodem die.
De Willelmo Stacy pro osmondo et alom. Valor: iiii^{xxx}iiii. Subsidium: iiii li. xiiii s.[252]
De Willelmo Spencer pro cupro. Valor: xvi li. xi s. viii d. Subsidium: xvi s. vii d.
Summa valoris istius navis: cx li. xi s. viii d. Subsidii: cx s. vii d.

Navis Willelmi Lauren applicuit ibidem eodem die.
De Jacobo SeintJorge pro patellis. Valor: xxxii li. viii s. iiii d. Subsidium: xxxii s. v d.
De Nicholao de Donnyngton pro for madre. Valor: viii li. Subsidium: viii s.
Summa valoris istius navis: xl li viii s. iiii d. Subsidii: xl s. v d.

Navis Henrici Keller applicuit ibidem eodem die.
De Nicholao Alford pro osmondo et madre. Valor: xlvi li. xviii s. ix d. Subsidium: xlvi s. xi d. ob.[253]
Summa valoris istius navis: paret. Subsidii: paret.

Navis Thome Andreuson applicuit ibidem eodem die.
De Johanne Appull pro heryngsmolt. Valor: x li. iiii s. Subsidium: x s. iii d.
De Roberto Messyngham pro wadda. Valor: xx li. Subsidium: xx s.
De Thoma Sprigg pro osmondo. Valor: lix li. xiii s. iiii d. Subsidium: lix s. viii d.
Summa valoris istius navis: iiii^{xx}ix li. xvii s. iiii d. Subsidii: iiii li. ix s. xi d.

Navis Severdi Gerardson applicuit ibidem vi die Octobris.
De Alberto van Heith pro pisce, oleo et clippyngg. Valor: ciiii^{xx}xviii li. vii s. vi. d. Subsidium: ix li.xviii s. iiii d. ob.[254]
De Bernardo Trowh pro pisce, oleo et clippyngg. Valor: clxx li. xv s. Subsidium: viii li x s. ix d.
De Henrico Semylouwh pro pisce et oleo. Valor: ciiii li. v s. Subsidium: ciiii s. iii d.
Summa valoris istius navis: ccccLxxiii li. vii s. vi d. Subsidii: xxiii li. xiii s. iiii d. ob.

Navis Hermanni Mynne applicuit ibidem edoem die.
De Hertwico Semne pro pisce, oleo et clippyngg. Valor: ciiii^{xx}xix li. xiii s. x. d. Subsidium: ix li. xix s. viii d. q.
De Egbarto Ravenesbergh pro pisce et oterfell. Valor: clxxvii li. v s. Subsidium: viii li. xvii s. iii d.

252 The controller's account omits 'et alom' from this entry.
253 The controller's account omits 'et madre' from this entry.
254 The controller's roll gives the value of the goods in this entry as £198 7s. 8d.

De Bernardo Knofflok pro pisce. Valor: cii li. xv s. Subsidium: cii s. ix d.
Summa valoris huius navis: ccccIxxxix li. xiii s x d. Subsidii: xxiii li. xix s. viii d. q.

Navis Nicholai Baser applicuit ibidem eodem die.
De eodem et marinariis suis pro pisce, oleo et bordis. Valor: xvii li. Subsidium: xvii s.
De Johanne Svenerlyng pro pisce et oleo. Valor: ciiii^{xx} li. xv s. ii d. Subsidium: ix li ix d. q.
Summa valoris huius navis: ciiii^{xx}xvii li. x s. ii d. Subsidii: ix li. xvii s. ix d. q.

Navis Jacobi Fowle applicuit ibidem eodem die.
De eodem et marinariis suis pro pisce et bordis. Valor: cxiiii li. xii s. Subsidium: cxiiii s. vii d. q.
De Hillario Wyghtman pro pisce et oleo. Valor: clxx li. Subsidium: viii li. x s.
De Hermanno van Hale pro pisce et clippyngg. Valor: xxx li. Subsidium: xxx s.
Summa valoris huius navis: cccxiiii li. xii s. Subsidii: xv li. xiiii s. vii d. q.

Navis Godkyni Wale applicuit ibidem eodem die.
De Johanne Feirwark pro pisce, oleo et clippyngg. Valor: cciiii^{xx}viii li. ix s. ii d. Subsidium: xiiii li. viii s. v d. ob.
De Bartholomeo van Stath pro pisce et oleo. Valor: ccclxxi li. xv s. Subsidium: xviii li. xi s. ix d.
De Bernardo Trowh pro pisce et clippyngg. Valor: ciiii^{xx}xvi li. v s. Subsidium: ix li. xvi s. iii d.
De Willelmo Leuencamp pro pisce et oleo. Valor: ccccxxv li. Subsidium: xxi li. v s.
Summa valoris huius navis: Mcciiii^{xx}i li.ix s. ii d. Subsidii: lxiiii li. xvii d. ob.

Navis Wassellini Weryng applicuit ibidem xv die Octobris.
De Hertwico Semne pro pisce. Valor: cciiii^{xx} li. xv s. Subsidium: xiiii li. ix d.
De Johanne Gronogh pro pisce. Valor: ciiii^{xx} li. x d. Subsidium: ix li. ob.
De Johanne Buxstote pro pisce. Valor; lx li. v s. Subsidium: lx s. iii d.
De Hermanno Housman pro pisce. Valor: lxviii li. Subsidium: lxviii s.
De Henrico Rodenbergh pro pisce valor: xix li. Subsidium: xix s.
Summa valoris huius navis: Dcviii li. x d. Subsidii: xxx li. viii s. ob.

Navis Willelmi Peeke applicuit ibidem eodem die.
De eodem at marinariis suis pro xii lastis allecis. Valor: xxxii li. xx d. Subsidium: xxxii s. i d.
De Wynkyno Brambergh pro xxxix lastis, xi barellis: cviii li.
Summa valoris huius navis: cxl li. xx d. Subsidii: vii li. i d.

Navis Walteri Bisshop applicuit ibidem eodem die.
De eodem et marinariis suis pro pisce. Valor: lxx li. Subsidium: lxx s.

De Rogero Paxman pro madre et patellis. Valor: lv li. Subsidium: lv s.
De Hermanno Braught pro calebere. Valor: iiii^{xx}vi li. v s. iiii d. Subsidium: iiii li. v s. iii d. q.
De Willelmo Martyn pro canevace. Valor: cxx li. Subsidium: vi li.
Summa valoris huius navis: cccxxxi li. v s. iiii d. Subsidii: xvi li. xi s. iii d. q.

Navis Johannis Dapper applicuit ibidem eodem die.
De Hugone de Wythome pro pipere et smigmate. Valor: lxii li. xviii s. viii d. Subsidium: lxii s. xi d. q.
De Johanne Sharp pro osmondo et cera. Valor: xl li. xv s. Subsidium: xl s. ix d.
De Johanne Bynglaye pro canevace. Valor: xxvi li. v s. Subsidium: xxvi s. iii d.
De Roberto de Wrangle pro smigmate. Valor: xl li. Subsidium: xl s.
Summa valoris istius navis: clxix li. xviii s. viii d. Subsidii: viii li. ix s. xi d. q.

Navis Frederici Farle applicuit ibidem xxx die Octobris.
De Henrico Skynkle pro pisce. Valor: cxxvi li. xi s. ii d. Subsidium: vi li. vi s. vi d. ob. q.
De Johanne Pape pro pisce et oleo. Valor: ciiii^{xx} li. v s. pro pisce et oleo. Subsidium: ix li. iii d.
De Ludberto Make pro pisce et oleo. Valor: clx li. xv s. Subsidium: viii li. ix d.
De Johanne Slotir pro pisce et oleo. Valor: clix li. Subsidium: vii li. xix s.
Summa valoris huius navis: Dcxxvi li. xi s. ii d. Subsidii: xxxi li. vi s. vi d. ob. q.

Navis Hermanni Growell applicuit ibidem eodem die.
De Johanne Rode for xi lastis et iii barellis allecis. Valor: xxx li. Subsidium: xxx s.
De Hertkyno Maryner pro vii lastis dimidio allecis. Valor: xx li. v s. Subsidium: xx s. iii d.
De Reynero Maryner pro xv lastis allecis. Valor: xl li. Subsidium: xl s.
De Jacobo Manne pro xviii lastis, ix barellis. Valor: l li. Subsidium: l s.
De Conrado Servaux pro ix lastis allecis et iiii lastis power: lxx li. Subsidium: lxx s.
De Johanne Servaux pro ix lastis dimidio allecis, viii barellis storgon: xl li. xiii s iiii d. Subsidium: xl s. viii d.
Summa valoris huius navis: ccl li. xviii s. iiii d. Subsidii: xii li. x s. xi d.

Navis Laurentii Claysson applicuit ibidem eodem die.
De eodem et marinariis suis pro ix lastis, ix barellis: xxvi li. xvi s. viii d. Subsidium: xxvi s. x d.
De Johanne Noldman pro xv lastis allecis: xl li. Subsidium: xl s.
De Bernardo Malthus pro xvi lastis dimidio, xx tymber wark: lx li. Subsidium: lx s.
De Philippo Baron pro xxvi lastis, iii barellis allecis: lxx li. Subsidium: lxx s.
De Fredericos de Flete pro xv lastis allecis: xl li. Subidium: xl s.
De Nicholao atte Green pro xi lastis, iii barellis: xxx li. Subsidium: xxx s.
Summa huius navis: cclxvi li. xvi s. viii d. Subsidii: xiii li. vi s. x d.

Navis Segbaldi Fure applicuit ibidem eodem die.
De Johanne Stephenson pro iii lastis, ix barellis. Valor: x li. Subsidium: x s.
De Johanne Hosyar pro vii lastis dimidio allecis. Valor: xx li. Subsidium: xx s.
De Petro Gernon pro xi lastis, iii barellis. Valor: xxx li. Subsidium: xxx s.
De Roberto Gybon pro iiii lastis dimidio allecis. Valor: xii li. Subsidium: xii s.
De Johanne Tenman pro v lastis, vii barellis allecis: xv li. Subsidium: xv s.
De Nicholao atte Green pro iiii lastis, viii barellis: xii li. xi s. viii d. Subsidium: xii s. vii d.
Summa valoris huis navis: iiii^{xx}xix li. xi s. viii d. Subsidii: iiii li. xix s. vii d.

Navis Tydekino Blok applicuit ibidem iiii die Novembris.
De eodem et marinariis suis pro xi lastis, iii barellis. Valor: xxx li. Subsidium: xxx s.
De Willelmo Hubard pro allecis, vii lastis dimidio. Valor: xx li. Subsidium: xx s.
De Willelmo Stephenson pro iii lastis, ix barellis: x li Subsidium: x s.
De Ricardo Ayleward pro vii lastis, vii barellis. Valor: xix li. v s. Subsidium: xix s. iii d.
Summa valoris huius navis: lxxix li. v s. Subsidii: lxxix s. iii d.

Navis Wallini Wastardeson applicuit ibidem eodem die.
De Reginaldo Reede pro vi lastis allecis. Valor: xvi li. vii d. Subsidium: xvi s. ob.
De Johanne Abraham pro vii lastis dimidio allecis. Valor: xx li. Subsidium: xx s.
De Ricardo Ayleward pro iiii lastis dimidio. Valor: xii li. Subsidium: xii s.
De Willelmo Halden pro vi lastis, ix barellis. Valor: xviii li. Subsidium: xviii s.
De Johanne Bell pro xi lastis, xi barellis. Valor: xxx li. Subsidium: xxx s.
Summa valoris huius navis: iiii^{xx}xvi li. vii d. Subsidii: iiii li xvi s. ob.

Navis Johanni Gulsogh applicuit ibidem edoem die.
De Roberto Chamberlein pro viii lastis allecis: xxii li. xi s. viii d. Subsidium: xx s. vii d.
De Johanne Bell pro xi lastis, iii barellis. Valor: xxx li. Subsidium: xxx s.
De Johannes Halydaye pro xi lastis, i barello. Valor: xxxi li. Subsidium: xxxi s.
De Bartholomeo Walsoken pro ix lastis, ix barellis. Valor: xxvi li. Subsidium: xxvi s.
Summa valoris huius navis: cix li. xi s. viii d. Subsidii: cix s. vii d.

Ex ista parte istius rotuli: vii^{M}Dcxli li. xiii s. v. Vinum: clxxv dolia, i pipa.

m. 7d.
Navis Johannis Kay exivit a portu predicto viii die Januarii anno quo infra.
De Johanne de Kirketon pro panno. Valor c li. Subsidium: c s.
De Rogero Harsyk, indigena, pro panno. Valor: xi li. xii s. viii d. Subsidium: cxi s. vii d. ob.
Summa valoris istius navis: cxi li. xii s. viii d. Subsidii: cxi s. vii d. ob.

Navis Laurentii Clayson exivit ibidem xxii die Januarii.
De edoem et marinariis suis pro frumento. Valor iiii^{xx} li xiiii s. Subsidium: iiii li. viii d. q.
De Petro Gernon pro frumento. Valor: xxxvi li. Subsidium: xxxvi s.
Summa valoris istius navis: cxvi li. xiiii s. Subsidii: cxvi s. viii d. q.

Navis Willelmi Barthagh exivit ibidem eodem die.
De Roberto Chamberlein pro frumento. Valor: xxi li. Subsidium: xxi s.
De Ruchero Sherman pro frumento. Valor: x li. xix s. iiii d. Subsidium: xi s.
Summa valoris istius navis: xxxi xix s. iiii d. Subsidii: xxxii s.

Navis Hermanni Mynne exivit ibidem xx die Februarii.
De Hermanno Housman pro panno. Valor: cciiii*xx*xix li. Subsidium: xiiii li. xix s.
De Johanne Hamele pro panno: cccc li. xvi s. x d. Subsidium: xx li. x s. ob.
De Waltero Scoupyng pro panno. Valor: Diiii^{xx} li. Subsidium: xix li.
De Hermanno Netle pro panno. Valor ccciiii*xx*xviii li. Valor: Subsidium: xix li. xviii s.
De Henrico Staynford pro panno. Valor: ccccIxxix li. Subsidium: xxiii li. xix s.
De Synerdo van Ferde pro panno. Valor: cccxlii li. Subsidium: xvii li. ii s.
Summa valoris istius navis: MMccciiii^{xx}xviii li. xvi s. x d. Subsidii: cxxiiii li. xviii s. x d. ob.

Navis Henrici Sounde exivit ibidem primo die Aprilis.
De Johanne Appull, indigena, pro panno. Valor: iiii^{xx}xii li. Subsidium: iiii li. xii s.
De Jacobo Seint Jeorge pro panno. Valor: clxvii. Subsidium: viii li. vii s.
De Johanne Haliday pro panno. Valor: ciiii li. ii s. x d. ob. Subsidium: ciiii s. ii d.
De Henrico de Kerle pro panno Valor: xxiiii li. Subsidium: xxiiii s.
De Hermanno Mynne pro panno. Valor: iiii^{xx}. Subsidium: iiii li.
Summa valoris istius navis: cccclxvii li. ii s. x d. ob. Subsidium: xxiii li. vii s. ii d.

Navis Wessellini Weryng exivit ibidem ultimo [die] Aprilis.
De Johanne van Heide pro panno. Valor: clxxviii li. Subsidium: viii li. xviii s.
De Johanne Slotir pro panno. Valor: ciiii^{xx}xix li. Subsidium: ix li. xix s.
De Tydekyno Luchogh pro panno. Valor: ccxix li. Subsidium: x li. xix s.
De Johanne van Heith pro panno. Valor: clxxix li. Subsidium: viii li. xix s.
De Johanne Strahenthorp pro panno. Valor: cciiii^{xxx}vi li. Subsidium: xiiii li. xvi s.
De Egbarto Ravensbergh pro panno. Valor: iiii^{xx}xvi li. xi s. i d. Subsidium: iiii li. xvi s. vii d.
Summa valoris istius navis: Mclxvii li. xi s. i d. Subsidii: lviii li. vii s. vii d.

Navis Hermanni Mynne exivit ibidem eodem die.
De Johanne Heith pro panno. Valor: cxxv li. xv s. ii d. Subsidium: vi li. v s. ix d. ob.
De Alberto Rainer pro panno. Valor: clx li. Subsidium: viii li.

De Ludekyno Heith pro panno. Valor: ciiii^{xx}xiiii. Subsidium: ix li. xiiii s.
De Johanne Pape pro panno. Valor: ciiii^{xx}i li. Subsidium: ix li. xii d.
Summa valoris istius navis: Dclx li. xv s. ii d. Subsidii: xxxiii li. ix d. ob.

Navis Ricardi Wagg' exivit versus Burdeux iiii die Augusti.[255]
De Reymondo Molyner [pro] frumento. Valor: viii li. ii. s vi d. Subsidium: viii s. i d. ob.
De Johanne Fawher pro frumento. Valor: cv s. Subsidium: v s. iii d.
Summa valoris istius navis: xiii li. vii s. vi d. Subsidii: xiii s. iiii d. ob.

Navis Ricardi Wasselyn exivit ibidem eodem die.
De Richero Sherman pro frumento. Valor: xix li. Subsidium: xix s.
De Willelmo Barthagh pro frumento: lx s. viii d. Subsidium: iii s. ob.
De Willelmo Draper pro frumento. Valor: vii li. vi s. viii d. Subsidium: vii s. iiii d.
Summa valoris istius navis: xxix li. vii s. iiii d. Subsidii: xxix s. iiii d. ob.

Navis Laurentii Clayson exivit ibidem quintodecimo die Augusti.
De Johanne Noldman pro panno. Valor: cciiii^{xx} li. xix s. Subsidium: xiiii li. xi d. ob.
De Willelmo Palmer pro panno. Valor: cxxxi li. viii s. Subsidium: vi li. xi s. v d.
De Johanne Abraham pro panno. Valor: cclxx li. Subsidium: xiii li. x s.
De Johanne Barfote pro panno. Valor: ciiii^{xx}v li. x s. Subsidium: ix li. v s. vi d.
De Nicholao de Donnyngton pro panno. Valor: cxliiii li. Subsidium: vii li. iiii s. vi d.
De Johanne de Preston pro panno. Valor: ccxi li. Subsidium: x li. xi s.
De Roberto Desterton pro panno. Valor: cx li. x s. Subsidium: cx s. vi d.
Summa valoris istius navis: Mccccxxxiii li. xvii s. Subsidii: lxvi li. xiii s. x d. ob.

Navis Segbaldi Fure exivit ibidem eodem die.
De Reginaldo Reed pro panno. Valor: iiii^{xx}x li. v s. Subsidium: iiii li. x s. iii d.
De Johanne Appull pro panno. Valor: ciiii^{xx}xii li. Subsidium: ix li. xii s.
De Johanne Huntstone pro panno. Valor: cxxxviii. Subsidium: vi li xviii s.
De Johanne Sawneby pro panno. Valor: iiii^{xx}x li. Subsidium: iiii li. x s.
De Henrico Kerle pro panno. Valor: cx li. Subsidium: cx s.
Summa valoris istius navis: Dcxx li. v s. Subsidii: xxxi li. iii d.

Navis Thomes Surflete exivit ibidem ix die Septembris versus Burdeux.
De Johanne Clerk pro frumento. Valor: xx li. x s. Subsidium: xx s. vi d.
De Johanne Harsyk pro frumento. Valor: xiiii li. x s. Subsidium: xiiii s. vi d.
Summa valoris istius navis: xxxv li. Subsidii: xxxv s.

---

255 The shipmaster's surname is given here in the abbreviated form used in the text.

Navis Rogeris atte Hous exivit ibidem versus Burdeux xiiii die Septembris.
De eodem pro frumento. Valor: x li. ii s. vi d. Subsidium: x s. i d. ob.
De Willelmo Gosberkirk pro frumento. Valor: xiiii li. Subsidium: xiiii s.
Summa valoris istius navis: xxiiii li. ii s. vi d. Subsidii: xxiiii s. i d. ob.

Navis Ricardi Bayouse exivit ibidem versus Burdeux xvi die Octobris.
De eodem et marinariis suis pro frumento. Valor: xxxi li. xvii s. viii d. Subsidium: xxx s. xi d. q.
De Johanne Fraunceys pro frumento. Valor: xxx li. Subsidium: xxx s.
De Peryno van Busse pro frumento. Valor: xx li. ii s. ii d. Subsidium: xx s. i d. q.
Summa valoris istius navis: iiii^{xx}ii li. xix s. x d. Subsidii: iiii li. ii s. ob.

Navis Johannis Rombald exivit versus Burdeux edoem die.
De eodem et marinariis suis pro frumento. Valor: xxi li. xvii s. viii d. ob. Subsidium: xxxvi s. x d. ob.
De Johanne Fraunceys pro frumento. Valor: xxx li. Subsidium: xxx s.
De Thoma Flayte pro frumento. Valor: xxx li. Subsidium: xxx s.
Summa valoris huius navis: iiii^{xx}xi li. xvii s. viii d. ob. Subsidii; iiii li. xi s. x d. ob.

Navis Godekyni Wale exivit ibidem xvii die Octobris.
De eodem pro panno. Valor: ciii s. iiii d. Subsidium: v s. ob.[256]
Summa: paret. Subsidii: paret.

Navis Petri Gernon exivit eodem die.
De Peryno del Busse pro frumento. Valor: xiii li. iii s. ix d. Subsidium: xiii s. ii d. q.
De Peryno del Garbboner pro frumento. Valor: xv li. Subsidium: xv s.[257]
Summa valoris istius navis: xxviii li. iii s. ix d. Subsidii: xxviii s. ii d. q.

Ista parte: vii^{M}iii^{c}xvii li. xv s. xi d.

Summa totalis rerum et vini:
Valor: xx^{M}Dccciii li. x s. Subsidium: Mxl li. iiii s. iid. Unde de incremento viii d. q.
Vini: ciiii^{xx}x doliis. Subsidium: xxviii li. x s.
Summa totalis receptionis denariorum: Mlxviii li. xiiii s. ii d. q.

256 At 12d. in the pound, this cloth should have paid 5s. 2d. subsidy.
257 The controller's roll gives this entry as 'De Peryno del Carboner'.

Glossary of commodities, measures and places included in T.N.A., E122/7/19

All':	can refer to herring (allecium) or garlic (allium). See note 248, above.
Allecium:	herring.
Allium:	garlic.
Alom:	alum.
Anguilla sals:	salted eel.
Asser:	sawn boards?
Barellus:	a measure of volume used here for herring and oil. For herring, a barrel usually contained 30 gallons; for oil, it usually contained 16 gallons. A barrel was usually one twelfth of a last.
Bitumen:	tar.
Borda:	boards.
Burdeux:	Bordeaux.
Calebere:	this term originally referred to a kind of squirrel skin ('calabre') from Calabria in Italy, but it was later applied more generally to a range of skins (Veale, *The English Fur Trade in the Later Middle Ages*, pp. 217–8). However, the entry in this account is for £86, a very large sum for furs, let alone for calaber, which was less valuable than Baltic squirrel skins, and so it may refer to steel (calabs).
Canevacium:	canvas.
Cepa:	onions.
Cera:	wax.
Clippyngg:	clipping, i.e. lamb-skin, shorn of wool and used for its hide.
Cuprum:	copper.
Dolium:	a tun, i.e. 252 gallons of wine or two pipes.
Ermyn:	ermine fells.
Ferrum:	iron.
Frumentum:	wheat.
Heryngsmolt:	herring smolt, i.e. young herring.
Lastum:	a measure of capacity used here for herring, herring smolt and power; the equivalent of twelve barrels.
Madre:	madder.
Nuces:	nuts.
Oleum:	fish-oil.

Osmondum:	osmund. Originally a superior quality of iron imported from the Baltic in small bars, but also applied to other iron sold in small bars or rods, or by the barrel or the sack, rather than by weight.
Oterfell:	otterfells.
Pannus:	woollen cloth.
Pannus lineus:	linen cloth.
Patella:	pan.
Pipa:	a pipe. Used here for half a tun of wine, i.e. 126 gallons.
Piscis:	fish. Used here for stockfish.
Power:	small herring or other fish.
Rosyn:	rosin. A substance obtained by the distillation of oil of turpentine from crude turpentine.
Sanctus Botulphus:	Boston.
Storgon:	sturgeon.
Tymber:	a timber, i.e. a bundle of forty furs.
Vinum:	wine.
Vinum de reno:	Rhenish wine.
Wadda:	woad.
Wark:	work, i.e. squirrel furs such as greywork.

Bibliography

Manuscript Sources

The National Archives, London.
DL29 Duchy of Lancaster, Ministers' Accounts.
E122 Exchequer K.R. Customs Accounts.
E159 Exchequer K.R. Memoranda Rolls.
E356 Exchequer L.T.R. Enrolled Customs Accounts.
E359 Exchequer L.T.R. Enrolled Lay Subsidy Returns.
E368 Exchequer L.T.R. Memoranda Rolls.

Printed Primary Sources

The Bolton Priory Compotus, 1286–1325, Together with a Priory Account Roll for 1377–1378, eds I. Kershaw, D. M. Smith and T. N. Cooper (Yorkshire Archaeological Society, Record Series, 154 (2000)).

British Borough Charters, 1307–1660, ed. M. Weinbaum (Cambridge, 1943).

Calendar of Close Rolls.

Calendar of Fine Rolls.

Calendar of Inquisitions Post Mortem.

Calendar of Patent Rolls.

Chester Customs Accounts, 1301–1566, ed. K. P. Wilson (Record Society of Lancashire and Cheshire, 111 (1969)).

The Customs Accounts of Hull, 1453–1490, ed. W. R. Childs (Yorkshire Archaeological Society, Record Series, 144 (1986 for 1984)).

The Customs Accounts of Newcastle-upon-Tyne, 1454–1500, ed. J. F. Wade (Surtees Society, 202 (1995)).

The Enrolled Customs Accounts, Parts 1–12, ed. S. Jenks (List and Index Society, volumes 303, 306–7, 313–14, 319, 324, 334, 341, 344–5, 348 (2004–13)).

Extracts from the Account Rolls of the Abbey of Durham, volume I, ed. J. T. Fowler (Surtees Society, 99 (1898)).

Letters and Papers, Foreign and Domestic, of the Reign of Henry VIII.

The London Customs Accounts: 24 Henry VI (1445/46), ed. S. Jenks (Cologne, 2018).

The Overseas Trade of Boston in the Reign of Richard II, ed. S. H. Rigby (Lincoln Record Society, 93, (2005)).

The Overseas Trade of Bristol in the Later Middle Ages, ed. E. M. Carus-Wilson (London, 1937)

The Overseas Trade of London: Exchequer Customs Accounts, 1480–1, ed. H. S. Cobb (London Record Society, 27 (1990)).

The Parliament Rolls of Medieval England, eds C. Given-Wilson et al., CD-ROM. Scholarly Digital Editions (Leicester, 2005).
The Poll Taxes of 1377, 1379 and 1381, Part 2: Lincolnshire-Westmoreland, ed. C. Fenwick (Oxford, 2001).
Rotuli Parliamentorum.
Statutes of the Realm, volume II (London, 1816).
Tudor Royal Proclamations, Volume I: The Early Tudors 91485–1553, eds P. L. Hughes and J. F. Larkin (New Haven, 1964).

Secondary Works

Allen, T. H., *The History of the County of Lincoln from the Earliest Period to the Present Time* (two volumes; London, 1834).
Amor, N. R., *From Wool to Cloth: The Triumph of the Suffolk Clothier* (Bungay, 2016).
Ayers, B., *The German Ocean: Medieval Europe Around the North* Sea (Sheffield, 2016).
Baker, R. L., 'The English customs service, 1307–43: a study of medieval administration', *Transactions of the American Philosophical* Society, n. s., 51/6 (1961), pp. 3–76.
Barron, C. M., *London in the Later Middle Ages: Government and People, 1200–1500* (Oxford, 2004).
Beardwood, A., *Alien Merchants in England, 1350 to 1377: Their Legal and Economic Position* (Cambridge, Mass., 1931).
Bell, A. R., Brooks, C. and Dryburgh, P. R., *The English Wool Market, c. 1230–1327* (Cambridge, 2007).
Blackmore, R., *Government and Merchant Finance in the Anglo-Gascon Trade, 1300–1500* (London, 2020).
Blake, J. L., 'Medieval smuggling in the north-east: some fourteenth-century evidence', *Archaeologia Aeliana*, fourth series, 48 (1965), pp. 243–60.
Bolton, J. L., 'Alien Merchants in England in the reign of Henry VI' (unpublished University of Oxford B.Litt. thesis, 1971).
Bonney, M., 'The English medieval wool and cloth trade—new approaches for the local historian', *The Local Historian*, 22/1 (1992), pp. 18–40.
Bridbury, A. R., *England and the Salt Trade in the Middle Ages* (Oxford, 1955).
Bridbury, A. R., 'English provincial towns in the later Middle Ages', *Economic History Review*, 34 (1981), pp. 1–24.
Britnell, R. H., *Britain and Ireland, 1050–1350: Economy and Society* (Cambridge, 2004).
Broadberry S., Campbell, B. M. S., Klein, A., Overton, M., van Leeuwen, B., *British Economic Growth, 1270–1870* (Cambridge, 2015).
Burkhardt, M., 'One hundred years of thriving commerce at a major English sea port: the Hanseatic trade at Boston between 1370 and 1470', in H. Brand and L. Müller, eds, *The Dynamics of European Culture in the North Sea and Baltic Region* (Hilversum, 2007), pp. 65–85.

Burkhardt, M., *Der hansische Bergenhandel in Spätmittelalter: Handel-Kaufleute-Netwerke* (Köln, 2009).

Burkhardt, M., 'The German Hanse and Bergen: new perspectives on an old subject', *Scandinavian Economic History Review*, 58 (2010), pp. 60–79.

Carus-Wilson, E. M., 'The medieval trade of the ports of the Wash', *Medieval Archaeology*, 6–7 (1962–3), pp. 182–201.

Carus-Wilson, E. M., *Medieval Merchant Venturers: Collected Studies* (second edition; London, 1967).

Carus-Wilson, E. M., and Coleman, O., *England's Export Trade, 1275–1547* (Oxford, 1963).

Cawthorne, P. M., 'Medieval Boston and the German Hanse (*c.*1250–1474)', in B. Ayers, *et al.*, *Six Essays in Hanseatic History* (Cromer, 2017), pp. 26–52.

Childs, W. R., *Anglo-Castilian Trade in the Later Middle Ages* (Manchester, 1978).

Childs, W. R., 'England's iron trade in the fifteenth century', *Economic History Review*, 34 (1981), pp. 25–47.

Childs, W. R., 'The English export trade in cloth in the fourteenth century', in R. Britnell and J. Hatcher, eds, *Progress and Problems in Medieval England: Essays in Honour of Edward Miller* (Cambridge, 1996), pp. 121–47.

Childs, W. R., 'Medieval English trade in the North Sea: Denmark and Jutland, *c* 1300–1500', in E. Damgaard, M. Guldberg and P. Holm, eds, *A North Sea Region: West Jutland and the World, II (Proceedings of the Lemvig Conference, April 3–5, 1995)* (Esbjerg, 1998), pp. 47–74.

Coleman, D. C., *The Economy of England, 1450–1750* (London, 1977).

Coleman, O., 'Trade and prosperity in the fifteenth century: some aspects of the trade of Southampton', *Economic History Review*, second series, 16 (1963–64), pp. 9–22.

Coleman, O., 'The collectors of customs in London under Richard II', in A. E. J. Hollaender and W. Kellaway, eds, *Studies in London History* (London, 1969), pp. 181–94.

Dollinger, P., *The German Hansa* (London, 1970).

Dyer, A., 'Ranking lists of English medieval towns', in D. M. Palliser, ed., *The Cambridge Urban History of Britain*, Volume I (Cambridge, 2000), pp. 747–70.

Fisher, F. J., 'Commercial trends and policy in sixteenth-century England', *Economic History Review*, 10 (1940), pp. 95–117.

Fryde, E. B., *Studies in Medieval Trade and Finance* (London, 1983).

Fudge, J. D., *Cargoes, Embargoes and Emissaries: The Commercial and Political Interaction of England and the German Hanse, 1450–1510* (Toronto, 1995).

Giles, K., 'St Mary's Guildhall, Boston, Lincolnshire: the archaeology of a medieval "public" building', *Medieval Archaeology*, 55 (2011), pp. 226–56.

Gras, N. S. B., *The Evolution of the English Corn Market from the Twelfth to the Eighteenth Century* (New York, 1915).

Gras, N. S. B., *The Early English Customs System* (Cambridge, Mass., 1918).

Gray, H. L., 'English foreign trade from 1446 to 1482', in E. Power and M. M. Postan, eds, *Studies in English Trade in the Fifteenth Century* (London, 1933), pp. 1–38, 361–3.

Gray, H. L., 'Tables of enrolled customs and subsidy accounts: 1399–1482', in E. Power and M. M. Postan, eds, *Studies in English Trade in the Fifteenth Century* (London, 1933), pp. 321–60.

Harden, G., *Medieval Boston and its Archaeological Implications* (Sleaford, 1978).

Harwood, W. A., 'The customs system in Southampton in the mid-fifteenth century', *Proceedings of the Hampshire Field Club and Archaeological Society*, 53 (1998), pp. 191–200.

Hatcher, J., *English Tin Production and Trade before 1500* (Oxford, 1973).

Haward, W. I., 'The trade of Boston in the fifteenth century', *Associated Architectural Societies Reports and Papers*, 41 (1932–33), pp. 169–78

Hill, J. W. F., *Medieval Lincoln*, (Stamford, 1990).

Hybel, N., 'The grain trade in northern Europe before 1350', *Economic History Review*, 55 (2002), pp. 219–47.

Jahnke, C., 'The Baltic trade', in D. J. Harreld, ed., *A Companion to the Hanseatic League* (Leiden, 2015), pp. 194–220.

James, M. K., 'A London merchant of the fourteenth century', *Economic History Review*, second series, 8 (1955–56), pp. 364–76,

James, M. K., *Studies in the Medieval Wine Trade*, ed. E. M. Veale, (Oxford, 1971).

Jenks, S., 'Zollamt, Häfen und Außenhandel in England: ca. 1377–1470', *Vierteljahresschrift für Sozial- und Wirtschaftsgeschichte*, 75 (1988), pp. 305–38.

Jenks, S., 'Die Carta Mercatoria. Ein hansisches Privileg', *Hansische Geschichtsblätter*, 108, (1990), pp. 45–86.

Jenks, S., *England, die Hanse und Preussen: Handel und Diplomatie* (three volumes; Cologne, 1992).

Jenks, S., 'Trade and relations between Lynn and the Hanse in the Middle Ages', in K. Friedland and P. Richards, eds, *Essays in Hanseatic History: The King's Lynn Symposium, 1998* (Dereham, 2005), pp. 94–114.

Jenks, S., 'Capturing opportunity, financing trade', in W. Blockmans, M. M. Krom and J. Wubs-Mrozewicz, eds, *The Routledge Handbook of Maritime Trade Around Europe, 1300–1600* (London, 2017), pp. 36–56.

Jones, E. T., *Inside the Illicit Economy: Reconstructing the Smugglers' Trade of Sixteenth-Century Bristol* (Abingdon, 2016).

Jones, M. K., and Underwood, M. G., *The King's Mother: Lady Margaret Beaufort, Countess of Richmond and Derby* (Cambridge, 1992).

Kerling, N. J., *Commercial Relations of Holland and Zeeland with England from the Late Thirteenth Century to the Close of the Middle Ages* (Leiden, 1954).

Kissane, A., *Civic Community in Medieval Lincoln: Urban Society and Economy in the Age of the Black Death, 1289–409* (Woodbridge, 2017).

Kowaleski, M., *Local Markets and Regional Trade in Medieval Exeter* (Cambridge, 1995).

Kowaleski, M., 'Port towns: England and Wales, 1300–1540', in D. M. Palliser, ed., *The Cambridge Urban History of Britain*, Volume I (Cambridge, 2000), pp. 467–94.

Lee, J. S., *The Medieval Clothier* (Woodbridge, 2018).

Lloyd, T. H., *The English Wool Trade in the Middle Ages* (Cambridge, 1977).

Lloyd, T. H., *Alien Merchants in England in the High Middle Ages* (Brighton, 1982).

Lloyd, T. H., *England and the German Hanse, 1157–1611: A Study of their Trade and Commercial Diplomacy* (Cambridge, 1991).

Minnis, J., and Carmichael, K., *Boston, Lincolnshire: Historic North Sea Port and Market Town* (Swindon, 2015).

Mitchell, B. R., *British Historical Statistics* (Cambridge, 1988).

Monckton, L., '"The beste and fayrest of al Lincolnshire": the parish church of St Botolph, Boston', in S. Badham and P. Cockerham, eds, *'The beste and fayrest of al Lincolnshire': The Church of St Botolph's, Boston, Lincolnshire, and its Medieval Monuments* (British Archaeological Reports, British Series, 554 (2012)), pp. 29–48.

Moore, E. W., *The Fairs of Medieval England: An Introductory Study* (Toronto, 1985).

Moorhouse, S., 'Finds in the refectory at the Dominican friary, Boston', *Lincolnshire History and Archaeology*, 7 (1972), pp. 21–53.

Munro, J. H., *Wool, Cloth and Gold: The Struggle for Bullion in Anglo-Burgundian Trade, 1340–1478* (Toronto, 1972).

Munro, J. H., 'The "industrial crisis" of the English textile towns, *c.*1290-*c.*1330', in M. Prestwich, R. Britnell and R. Frame, eds, *Thirteenth Century England, VII: Proceedings of the Durham Conference, 1997* (Woodbridge, 1999), pp. 103–42.

Munro, J. H., 'Scarlet', in G. R. Owen-Crocker, E. Coatsworth and M. Hayward, eds, *Encyclopedia of Dress and Textiles in the British Isles, c.450*–1450 (Leiden, 2012), pp. 476–81.

Nedkvitne, A., *The German Hansa and Bergen, 1100–1600* (Bergen, 2014).

Oldland, J. R., 'The expansion of London's overseas trade from 1475 to 1520', in C. M. Barron and A. F. Sutton, eds, *The Medieval Merchant: Proceedings of the 2012 Harlaxton Symposium* (Donington, 2014), pp. 55–92.

Oldland, J. R., 'London's trade in the time of Richard III', *The Ricardian*, 24 (2014), pp. 1–30.

Oldland, J. R., *The English Woollen Industry, c.1200–1560* (Abingdon, 2019).

Ormrod, W. M., 'The English Crown and the customs', *Economic History Review*, 40 (1987), pp. 27–40.

Ormrod, W. M., *The Reign of Edward III: Crown and Political Society, 1327–1377* (London, 1990).

Ormrod, W. M., 'Government by commission: the continual council of 1386 and English royal administration', *Peritia*, 10 (1996), pp. 303–321

Ormrod, W. M., 'The origins of tunnage and poundage: parliament and the estate of merchants in the fourteenth century', *Parliamentary History*, 28 (2009), pp. 209–27.

Postan, M. M., 'The economic and political relations of England and the Hanse from 1400 to 1475', in E. Power and M. M. Postan, eds, *Studies in English Trade in the Fifteenth Century* (London, 1933), pp. 91–153.

Power, E., 'The wool trade in the fifteenth century', in E. Power and M. M. Postan, eds, *Studies in English Trade in the Fifteenth Century* (London, 1933), pp. 39–90.

Power, E., *The Wool Trade in Medieval English History* (Oxford, 1941).

Ramsey, P., 'Overseas trade in the reign of Henry VII: the evidence of customs accounts', *Economic History Review*, second series, 6 (1953–4), pp. 173–182.

Rickert, E., 'Extracts from a fourteenth-century account book', *Modern Philology*, 24 (1926–27), pp. 111–19, 249–56.

Rigby, S. H., 'Boston and Grimsby in the Middle Ages' (unpublished University of London Ph.D. thesis, 1983).

Rigby, S. H., 'Boston and Grimsby in the Middle Ages: an administrative contrast', *Journal of Medieval History*, 10 (1984), pp. 51–66.

Rigby, S. H., 'The customs administration at Boston in the reign of Richard II', *Bulletin of the Institute of Historical Research*, 58 (1985), pp. 12–24.
Rigby, S. H., '"Sore decay" and "fair dwellings": Boston and urban decline in the later Middle Ages', *Midland History*, 10 (1985), pp. 47–61.
Rigby, S. H., *Medieval Grimsby: Growth and Decline* (Hull, 1993).
Rigby, S. H., '"John of Gaunt's Palace" and the Sutton family of Lincoln', *Lincolnshire History and Archaeology*, 35 (2000), pp. 35–9.
Rigby, S. H., 'Urban population in late medieval England: the evidence of the lay subsidies', *Economic History Review*, 63 (2010), pp. 393–417.
Rigby, S. H., 'Medieval Boston: economy, society and administration', in S. Badham and P. Cockerham, eds, *'The beste and fayrest of al Lincolnshire': The Church of St Botolph's, Boston, Lincolnshire, and its Medieval Monuments* (British Archaeological Reports, British Series, 554 (2012)), pp. 6–28.
Rigby, S. H., *Boston, 1086–1225: A Medieval Boom Town* (Lincoln, 2017).
Rose, S., *The Wine Trade in Medieval Europe, 1000–1500* (London, 2011).
Rose, S., *The Wealth of England: The Wool Trade and its Political Importance, 1100–1600* (Oxford, 2017).
Ross, C., *Edward IV* (New Haven, 1997).
Sapoznik, A., 'Bees in the medieval economy: religious observance and the production, trade and consumption of wax in England, c.1300–1555', *Economic History Review*, 72 (2019), pp. 1152–74.
Sarnowsky, J., 'The "Golden Age" of the Hanseatic League', in D. J. Harreld, ed., *A Companion to the Hanseatic League* (Leiden, 2015), pp. 64–100.
Saul, N., *Richard II* (New Haven, 1997).
Schanz, G., *Englische Handelspolitik gegen Ende des Mittelalters mit besonderer Berücksichtigung des Zeitalters der beiden ersten Tudors Heinrich VII und Heinrich VIII* (two volumes, Leipzig, 1881).
Slavin. P., 'The great bovine pestilence and its economic and environmental consequences in England and Wales, 1318–50', *Economic History Review*, 65 (2012), pp. 1239–66.
Slavin, P., 'Mites and merchants: the crisis of English wool and textiles revisited', *Economic History Review*, 73 (2020), pp. 885–913.
Steel, A., 'The collectors of customs at Newcastle-upon-Tyne in the reign of Richard II', in J. Conway Davies, ed., *Studies Presented to Sir Hilary Jenkinson* (London, 1957), pp. 380–413.
Steel, A., 'The collectors of customs in the reign of Richard II', in H. Hearder and H. Loyn, eds, *British Government and Administration* (Cardiff, 1974), pp. 27–39.
Swanson, R. N., *Indulgences in Late Medieval England: Passports to Paradise?* (Cambridge, 2007).
Thompson, P., 'On the early commerce of Boston', *Associated Architectural Societies Reports and Papers*, 2 (1852–3), pp. 362–81.
Thompson, P., *The History and Antiquities of Boston* (Boston, 1856).
Unger, R. W., 'The Netherlands herring fishery in the later Middle Ages: the false legend of William Beukels of Biervliet', *Viator*, 9 (1978), pp. 335–56.
Veale, E. M., *The English Fur Trade in the Later Middle Ages* (Oxford, 1966).
Watts, J., *Henry VI and the Politics of Kingship* (Cambridge, 1996).

Index